Cambridge Studies in Islamic Civilization

Unlawful gain and legitimate profit in Islamic law

An interest-free banking system has recently been adopted by several countries to operate in parallel with the existing world banking system. This comprehensive guide to the newly re-asserted system, a subject of practical concern for all involved in international trade between Western and Muslim countries, sets on a new footing contemporary discussion of risk and profit in an Islamic context.

Nabil Saleh examines two restrictive rules in Islamic law, reflected in the ban on taking interest and the rejection of aleatory contracts, which strongly conflict with the existing world banking system. The re-assertion of Islamic law in a coherent banking system is considered in the context of its international legal implications. The book is also a comparative study of the two rules in five schools of law, as all aspects are examined in the light of the teaching of the four Sunni schools which hold authority in the Arab states and in Pakistan and of the Ibadi school of law peculiar to Oman.

Cambridge Studies in Islamic Civilization

Titles in the series

ANDREW M. WATSON. *Agricultural innovation in the early Islamic world: the diffusion of crops and farming techniques 700–1100*

ELIAS N. SAAD. *Social history of Timbuktu: the role of Muslim scholars and notables 1400–1900*

G. H. A. JUYNBOLL. *Muslim tradition: studies in chronology, provenance and authorship of early ḥadīth*

BASIM MUSALLAM. *Sex and society in Islam: birth control before the nineteenth century*

SURAIYA FAROQHI. *Towns and townsmen of Ottoman Anatolia: trade craft and food production in an urban setting, 1520–1650*

Unlawful gain and legitimate profit in Islamic law

Riba, *gharar* and Islamic banking

NABIL A. SALEH

Cambridge University Press
Cambridge
London New York New Rochelle
Melbourne Sydney

Published by the Press Syndicate of the University of Cambridge
The Pitt Building, Trumpington Street, Cambridge CB2 1RP
32 East 57th Street, New York, NY 10022, USA
10 Stamford Road, Oakleigh, Melbourne 3166, Australia

First published 1986

Printed in Great Britain at the University Press, Cambridge

British Library cataloguing in publication data

Saleh, Nabil A.
Unlawful gain and legitimate profit in Islamic law: riba, gharar and Islamic banking.——(Cambridge studies in Islamic civilization)
1. Banks and banking——Islamic countries
I. Title
332.1.'0917'671 HG3368

Library of Congress cataloguing in publication data

Saleh, Nabil A.
Unlawful gain and legitimate profit in Islamic law.
(Cambridge studies in Islamic civilization)
Bibliography: p.
Includes index.
1. Interest (Islamic law) 2. Risk (Islamic law)
3. Sales (Islamic law) 4. Banking law (Islamic law)
I. Title. II. Series.
LAW 297'.14 85-25547

ISBN 0 521 32298 7

WV

To my friend Ghassan I. Shaker
with esteem and affection

Contents

Foreword *page* xi

Introduction: the Islamic economic order 1
Saudi Arabia 5
Kuwait 5

1 *Riba* (unlawful advantage by way of excess or deferment) 8
1 The background of the Quranic prohibition 8
Earlier views on interest 8
The Quranic doctrine 9
2 Definitions 12
Riba 13
Genus and species 13
ʿIlla 14
3 Various interpretations of *ʿilla* and genus 15
ʿIlla 15
Genus 16
4 Traditional views on *riba* 19
Hanafis 19
Shafiis 21
Hanbalis 22
Malikis 24
Ibadis 26
5 Other views on *riba* 26
Ibn ʿAbbas 26
Ibn Qayyim 27
ʿAbduh and Rida 28
Sanhuri 28
Daoualibi 29
Shaikh Draz 29
Zaydan Abu al-Karim Hassan 30

6 *Ribawi* transactions with non-Muslims 30
Appendix 1 Sources of the prohibition of *riba* 33

2 *Qard* (loan of fungible commodities) 35
1 *Qard* and *riba* 35
2 Repayment of a *qard* according to *fiqh* 37
What should be repaid to the lender, and where? 37
Is the lender entitled to derive any advantage from the *qard*? 41
3 *Qard* with a *riba* stipulation: valid or not? 44
4 *Riba*'s narrowed scope 47

3 *Gharar* (uncertainty, risk, speculation) 49
1 Introduction 49
2 Definition of *gharar* 50
3 Avoiding want of knowledge (*jahl*) concerning the existence of the exchanged countervalues 52
The subject-matter in bilateral transactions 52
The effects of *gharar* on gratuitous contracts and unilateral transactions 56
Donation 56
Wills 57
Power of attorney 57
Sale of fruits and agricultural products 59
*Istisna*ʿ (contract of manufacture) 61
The price 62
4 Avoiding want of knowledge (*jahl*) concerning the characteristics and quantities of the exchanged countervalues, and the date of future performance 63
Payment unavailable at the parties' meeting 65
Subject-matter unavailable at the parties' meeting: (1) *bay*ʿ *gha'ib* 67
Subject-matter unavailable at the parties' meeting: (2) *bay*ʿ *salam* 71
Sale where subject-matter or price may be determined by viewing: *bay*ʿ *juzaf* 76
5 Keeping effective control over the exchanged countervalues 79
Subject-matter 79
Price 80
Appendix 2 Sources of the prohibition of *gharar* 85

4 A financial system based on Islamic ethics 86
1 A short survey 86
The Islamic financial institutions 90

2 The operations traditional to *fiqh* revived by Islamic financial institutions 91
Musharaka or *sharika* 91
Murabaha 94
Expenses in relation to *murabaha* 95
Options when *murabaha* prices prove to be inflated 96
Ijara 97
Ijara wa-iqtina' 99
Qard hasan 99
Takaful 100
3 The *mudaraba* (commenda partnership) 101
Definition 103
Mudaraba capital 104
Investor's duties and rights 106
Agent-manager's duties and rights 109

Conclusion: the unique character of the Sharia Law of Contract and the prospects for success of an Islamic banking system 115

Glossary 119

Bibliography 123

Index 127

Foreword

This is not a book about the more sensational aspects of the Islamic legal system as seen through the Western media. Issues of far greater significance and much more widespread effect are involved in the current process of Islamisation of the law in Muslim countries – the stamping of the law with a peculiarly Islamic identity. In the civil law of obligations, particularly business contracts, there are many fundamental issues which have a deep-rooted significance for the Muslim religious conscience. This is especially so in regard to commercial profit and loss, because this involves the long-standing Islamic abhorrence of interest from capital investment and of speculative transactions of risk. Now, at last, we have here, for the first time in the English language, an in-depth examination of these core problems of commercial law, covering both the traditional doctrine of the ancient legal sources and the practical attitudes and approaches arising therefrom in the modern expression of the law.

It is not, however, the purpose of a foreword to review a book but rather simply to introduce it and its author to the reader. This I do, readily and happily, as one who has been a professional colleague and friend of the author for a good number of years. Academically Nabil Saleh is soundly qualified in both "Western" law – he is a graduate of the Beirut Law School – and Islamic law – he studied Sharia under the eminent authority Subhi Mahmasani – and he has combined the two in his legal practice. In particular he was instrumental in drafting, *inter alia*, the Omani Commercial Companies Law which he analyses in his book *Saudi Arabian and Omani Company Laws*. Here he also demonstrates clearly his exhaustive command and understanding of the original Arabic sources of the Sharia. Post-graduate law students at London have greatly benefited from the seminars at which he has been invited to speak on the general topic of commercial laws of the Middle East. On these occasions it has always seemed to me that, in his thoughtful remarks and temperate arguments, always advanced with a congenial sense of humour and humanity, his audience has observed the real personality of the man himself.

It is a trite assertion that Islamic law is a God-given and religious legal system as opposed to the secular man-made legal systems of the West; but the manifold and far reaching implications of this distinction are often not fully appreciated. Commercial law, for example, in the West is orientated towards the intrinsic needs of sound economics, such as stability of obligation and certitude of promised performance. In the religious law of Islam, on the other hand, equitable considerations of the individual conscience in matters of profit and loss override the technicalities of commercial dealings. It is the harmonization of these two very different approaches which poses the real challenge for developing Islamic law today.

Nabil Saleh defines and squarely faces up to this fundamental challenge as he deals with the details of financial transactions. I am confident that the reader will enjoy as I myself have done, this clear exposition, in a style hallmarked by moderation and objectivity, of a very complicated and important topic by one of recognized and mature expertise in Middle Eastern law both as a practising consultant and as a legal scholar.

Noel Coulson

Professor of Oriental Laws
and Dean of Laws in the
University of London

Introduction

The realization that the Prophet had in mind the establishment of a secular order where the teaching of his revelation would be put into practice came slowly, but eventually the Meccans understood this message. The selfishness of the rich and powerful was denounced. The assertion of the oneness of the God in the name of whom Muhammad was preaching prevented His name being added to the vast panoply of gods already worshipped in Mecca. Various attempts at accommodation were made but failed. No room for compromise was left either in this world or in the world hereafter, and it became obvious that the established structure of the city of Mecca was in real jeopardy. Persecution of the Prophet and his followers gradually increased until a boycott was imposed on the Banu Hashim to whom Muhammad belonged, although to resort to such an extreme was not a decision taken lightly by any seventh-century Arabian clan. When the persecution became so intense that the Prophet feared for his life and that of the converts to Islam, he took refuge in another city of the Hijaz called at that time Yathrib (later to be called Madinat al-Nabi, "city of the Prophet", or for short Medina), which witnessed the first settlement of an Islamic community.

Most of the Islamic dictates and prohibitions regarding secular transactions and human relationships were revealed during the Medinan period, when the Islamic community had a chance to express itself freely, but the Meccan period was not devoid of secular prescriptions (for example, the prohibition of hoarding wealth, Quzan s. CIV:1–4), and the seed of many such prescriptions germinated in Mecca before finding full expression in Medina, for example the gradual prohibition of drinking wine and dealing in *riba*.[1] The Prophet's anathemata, which could have been ignored or at least taken more lightly by his normally sceptical compatriots, if they had been solely concerned with spiritual life, instead worried them deeply. Such apprehension was justified, for the Quran and the Sunna[2] form a code of religious tenets and worldly prescriptions a peculiar feature of which is that

[1] *Riba* is usually translated as "interest" or "usurious interest"; in fact it has a much wider meaning (see p. 13 below).

[2] Deeds, utterances and unspoken approvals of the Prophet.

frequently a value judgment which seemed at first to relate only to the souls of believers was transformed at the first opportunity into a prescription of mandatory application. So, for example, while the Quran stresses the practice of *zakat* (alms tax) as one of the chief virtues of believers (cf. s. XIII:22; s. XXXV:29; s. LXX:24ff. and s. LXXVI:8ff. – all of the Meccan period), the Medinan period witnessed the transformation of a commendable virtue into one of the fundamental duties of Muslims.[3] In the same manner the first verses concerning the drinking of wine and dealing in *riba* were revealed in Mecca in the form of a mere moral exhortation. The straightforward condemnation came later in Medina.[4] It is therefore no surprise that the objectives of Sharia (the sacred law of Islam) pertain not only to the afterlife but also to this world. These dual objectives were summed up by the great Hanbali theologian of the fourteenth century, Ibn Qayyim al-Jawziyya,[5] as being the welfare of people in this world as well as in the hereafter, this welfare comprising complete justice, mercy, well-being and wisdom. Ghazali, the eminent philosopher of Islam, has defined the Sharia objectives as safeguarding, for human beings, their faith, their life, their intellect, their posterity and their property.[6]

Because one of the prime duties of man is to conduct his life in accordance with the will of Allah, the means of attaining the objectives of Sharia, whether mundane or spiritual, must be Islamically legitimate and consequently dominated by ethics. Moreover, if one definition of economics is that of a science whose chief purpose is to investigate the effects of various economic phenomena and to define the ways which will assist in providing welfare, then economic order is necessarily among these means and ought to be, according to Muslim thinkers, Islamic: that is, it should derive from the ethical norms of Islam. Islamic economic order should strive, as stated in the words of a Muslim economist, to build bridges between the "is" and the "ought".[7] This economic order envisaged by Muslim contemporary economists is based on a positive line of action leading towards the ultimate aim of welfare dispensed with justice and equity and tempered by wisdom – these can be considered the spiritual and philosophical facets of the Islamic economic concept. At the same time, the chosen line of action should be confined within boundaries defined by certain prohibitory rules which give that concept a moral and religious outlook.

While Muslim scholars are in agreement as to what these prohibitory rules are, they have yet to decide on one positive line of action. That their views are so diverse is a healthy sign of the seriousness of their studies. Some contemporary Muslim authors see in state intervention in the banking

[3] H. A. R. Gibb and J. H. Kramers (eds.), *Shorter Encyclopaedia of Islam*, s.v. Zakat.
[4] Shaikh Draz, "L'usure en droit musulman", pp. 147–8.
[5] *I'lam al-muwaqqi'in*, Vol. III, p. 4.
[6] al-Ghazali, *al-Mustasfa*, Vol. I, pp. 130–40.
[7] M. N. Siddiqi, *Muslim Economic Thinking*, p. 69.

system itself the ideal way to eliminate interest and other unlawful gains.[8] The overwhelming majority see the solution mainly in a profit-sharing system to replace interest.[9] A few still question the relevance of any of the proposed solutions and ask Muslim economists to continue their research and experiments so as to discover an Islamic avenue to economic development.[10]

This book is chiefly concerned with the main prohibitory rules which are unanimously acknowledged, in principle at least, by Muslims; these are the rules referring to *riba* (unlawful advantage by way of excess or deferment) and *gharar* (uncertainty, risk and speculation). It is also concerned with interest-free banking and *mudaraba* (commenda partnership), not only because the *mudaraba* technique for the distribution of profits and losses is adopted by the vast majority of contemporary Muslim economists as the principal substitute for interest, but also because it is actually and widely put into practice by most Islamic financial institutions which consider profit-sharing as the foundation of their operations. It should be stressed, however, that it is law and not economics which is the subject of this book.

Riba, *gharar* and *mudaraba* are explained and defined at a later stage, for this is better done in the course of examining the details of each of these concepts; otherwise the risk of conveying wrong or incomplete meaning is too great. One point that should be made here is that the rules on *riba* and *gharar*, or at least their too strict implementation, have long been alleged to be the major impediment to the evolution of Islamic jurisprudence in line with the requirements of modern life.[11] Yet it is only fair to emphasize that, when the principal author of the draft of the Egyptian Civil Code made his statement (in the 1950s), it was impossible to foresee any change in the Western-inspired financial and economic systems in force in the Islamic countries. That probably explains the severe judgment expressed by Sanhuri, who had witnessed for too long the two unbending prohibitory Sharia rules in perpetual conflict with an established order which spurned them.

Now a change is under way; powerful groups of thinkers and financiers from different Islamic countries have shown a strong determination to establish an economic order that is in line with the teaching of Islam. Many among these groups are aware that "the sole abolition of *riba* is not powerful enough by itself to engineer a smooth transition from an interest-laden economic system to an exploitation-free Islamic economy".[12] Avoiding *gharar* in transactions is recommended, but as part of a new economic method where the prohibition of *riba* and *gharar* is no longer an impediment

[8] S. N. H. Naqvi, *Ethics and Economics, an Islamic Synthesis*, pp. 112 and 122; Khalid A. Ahmad, *al-Tafkir al-iqtisadi*, pp. 48f.

[9] Siddiqi, *Muslim Economic Thinking*, pp. 30–1.

[10] Khurshid Ahmad, "Economic development in an Islamic framework", pp. 171–2.

[11] ‘Abd al-Razzaq Sanhuri, *Masadir al-haqq fi ’l-fiqh al-islami*, Vol. III, p. 14.

[12] Naqvi, *Ethics and Economics*, p. 153.

but a guideline. Have *mudaraba* and other Islamic concepts enough leverage to reassert themselves as workable devices? Time alone will tell. What is certain today is that the challenge is no longer a theoretical one.

This change pursued by the Islamic intelligentsia is not the result of abstract thinking but mainly the product of a collective feeling that most Asian and African Muslims have shared for more than a decade. What they sense and desire is that Sharia should guide and govern their lives from the cradle to the grave and should not be confined to family matters as it has been under what they saw as a premeditated plan concocted by Western powers at a time when most Islamic states and communities were under foreign domination. The result is that there is a growing impetus for fresh evaluation and new interpretation of original Sharia principles, with the aim of reasserting Sharia as a valid and sensible corpus of commercial and civil laws.

Besides a genuine religious conviction that cannot legitimately be denied, Muslims see their religion as the generator of an original and rich civilization and the guide for a righteous way of life, and see no reason why it should not regain the overall position it had before nearly fading away under foreign pressure. Religion is deemed to have played a large part in assisting affluent countries to reach the comfortable position they enjoy, while for the less fortunate religion is a comfort and offers a unique chance to escape from a grim reality.

As is more or less inevitable when changes of heart and mind of such magnitude occur in society, an extremist fundamentalist movement acquired a renewed momentum in some Islamic states. Such movements preach the return to the basic values and sources of Islam as taught in the golden past but reject evaluation and interpretation which bend to modern exigencies. Whether the moderate current or the more extremist one will prevail, the examination of the sources of *riba* and *gharar* cannot be neglected, for in either event Sharia will increasingly evolve as an integral element of the business laws of the Islamic states, if it is not already the established norm.

The pertinent question at this stage is whether there is enough room in the present legal systems of these states and in the practice they follow to accommodate the Sharia principles governing *riba* and *gharar*. Two Arab states have been selected here to provide us with an answer: Saudi Arabia and Kuwait, chosen because each represents one of the two main legal structures governing secular transactions in the Arab states – religious and family matters not being our direct concern.

One legal system follows Sharia and is in effect in countries such as Saudi Arabia, the Yemen Arab Republic (North Yemen) and Oman. Sharia in these countries maintains a dominant position, although they are governed by different schools of law (Saudi Arabia complies with Hanbali teaching; in Oman the Ibadi sect is prevalent; and in North Yemen the Zaidi and Shafii schools), and although each of these countries has adopted a substantial number of secular statutes borrowed from Western laws and more particularly French law through the channel of Egyptian and Lebanese draftsmen, and that curtails to some extent the ascendancy of Sharia. Characteristically, Saudi Arabia and Oman have not enacted a Civil Code, Sharia serving that purpose, whereas the Yemen Arab Republic has recently (1979) adopted one entirely based on Sharia, to such an extent that it may be safely described as a contemporary compendium of Islamic rules and principles. With the other legal system, Sharia plays a part which varies from small in countries such as Syria and Tunisia, to moderate in Qatar, Kuwait and Bahrain, although the pressure of champions for complete adherence to Sharia is on the increase everywhere.

Saudi Arabia

Paying and receiving interest on bank deposits, loans or negotiable instruments and generally speaking all sorts of *ribawi* transactions are theoretically prohibited in Saudi Arabia under the governing Hanbali school (for more detail on *riba* as taught by the Hanbalis, see below, pp. 22ff.). In the same manner all contracts based on chance, or contracts which contain a material element of *gharar* (uncertainty, risk, speculation) are unlawful under the same teaching. Notwithstanding the fact that neither the Saudi Companies Regulation nor any other regulation specifically prohibits the setting up of an insurance business (a typical example of contract based on chance), no firm, whether wholly or partly Saudi-owned, can obtain commercial registration to carry on the insurance business. Moreover, a number of statutory laws (called Regulations in Saudi Arabia, to emphasize that Allah alone gives law) contain clauses declaring that dealing with interest is unlawful (see for example Art. 6 of Regulation no. 37 of 1383 A.H. on Negotiable Instruments, and Arts. 2 and 6 of the Saudi Arabian Monetary Agency Regulation no. 23 of 1376 A.H.). That is the law, and definitively Saudi courts will not entertain claims with respect to interest, or claims based on *riba* and *gharar*. But dealing with interest is common practice, and insurance business in Saudi Arabia thrives. All of that is unlawful, but not actionable; it is merely tolerated out of necessity and under the exigencies of international business. But this should not be considered a permanent departure from the rules. At any moment, the prohibition of *riba* and *gharar* may be reinstated, with full and comprehensive effects.

Kuwait

Kuwait enacted a Civil Code on 1 October 1980 that came into force on 25 February 1981, the Independence Day of Kuwait. Until then, Kuwait's Civil Code was the Majalla and Book Two of the Commercial Code of 1961 labelled "Obligations in General", which, together with the entire Commercial Code of 1961, was repealed by a new Commercial Code promulgated in 1980, also with effect from 25 February 1981. The new Civil Code of 1980 is inspired by the Egyptian Civil Code of 1949 and contains and takes into acount a certain number of Sharia principles which at times seem not to blend smoothly into a piece of legislation mainly inspired by the French legal system, or even to be consistent with other Kuwaiti statutes. *Riba* and *gharar* are among the Sharia principles referred to, as the examples set out below indicate.

The new Civil Code pays tribute to Sharia by prescribing that the subject-matter of an obligation should be determined in a way which dispels an undue want of knowledge, so that whenever the obligation is in respect of a tangible object, the said object should be designated individually or by its species, amount and degree of quality, otherwise the contract which has generated the obligation is null and void (Art. 171). But when the same code allows scope for courts to calculate, when assessing compensation, the loss of profit sustained by the creditor of an obligation (Art. 300), it is clear that the prohibition of *gharar* is disregarded. This is instanced by Law no. 24 of 1961 on Insurance Companies and Agents.

Interest has suffered the same fate as *gharar*. On the one hand it is plainly stipulated in the Civil Code of 1980 that a loan should be discharged with the same species characteristics and quantum (Art. 543) and also that a loan cannot generate interest or secure an advantage to the lender (Art. 547), two Sharia principles intended to avert *riba* and *gharar*; on the other hand we find in the same Code that courts are entitled, when an uncommon damage is proved, to grant the creditor of a monetary obligation an equitable compensation for the loss originated by the debtor's resistance to performing his obligation (Art. 306). It is also true that the Central Bank of Kuwait fixes by law the minimum and maximum rates of interest on deposits.

The inconsistencies found between Sharia and practice, and between Sharia principles embodied in contemporary enactments and other provisions of the same enactments were not, until recently, of too much concern to the legal profession or to litigants. In fact, only a few years ago the dichotomy in each of the two legal systems – that of Kuwait and that of Saudi Arabia – was little felt. The reason is that Sharia was given in most Arab states and in business as practised a lesser role than formally acknowledged. In other words, Sharia was paid lip-service in various Western-inspired pieces of legislation while being most of the time confined to family matters and religious affairs. This is no longer the case, for various reasons pertaining to newly acquired independence, religious revival and political options: Sharia today claims at least the position that words, if not deeds, concede it in those places where it is not a dominant position voiced by fundamentalism.

Whether or not Sharia will be reasserted as the only source of the law or as a basis for supplying rules in the absence of relevant ones in the statutory provisions and for the interpretation of the statutory provisions themselves, the examination of the sources of *riba* and *gharar* according to the four Sunni schools which hold authority in the Arab States and to the Ibadi school of law peculiar to Oman, is of increasing practical importance.

CHAPTER 1

Riba (unlawful advantage by way of excess or deferment)

I The background of the Quranic prohibition

Earlier views on interest

It is reasonable to assume that some sense of property, whether inborn or inculcated, inclined our prehistoric ancestors not to part with any of the goods they owned without a satisfactory compensation, which necessarily took the form of an exchange with other goods. It is not known how and when those ancestors became aware of the intangible value of their coveted goods and asked for an addition to the bare value. We can only imagine that they passed from the stage of an even-handed barter to business fairly rapidly. Lenders must have followed the same progression, starting with the desire to have back exactly what was remitted to the borrowers, then attaining the stage where they wished to secure extra gain, and later on regular interest, upon what was lent.

The lawfulness of such additional return, or at least its moral aspect, is still discussed. Under religious and social pressures a distinction was made in most places, virtually from the outset, between lawful interest and unlawful usury. Such a distinction might well be relevant to a certain place at a certain time, but sooner or later, and with inevitable change of circumstances, there is every prospect that it would be considered as an arbitrary criterion. Nevertheless there has been admirable persistence on the part of secular and spiritual leaders in trying to measure and regulate the ever elusive question of lawful interest.

Written history tells us that compound interest was forbidden by the Code of Hammurabi (Article 93 of this code issued *c.* 1750 B.C.) and that King Bocchoris of the Egyptian 24th Dynasty (*c.* 730 – *c.* 715 B.C.) forbade the taking of interest in excess of the principal. As pointed out by Sanhuri, destiny decreed that after three thousand years Egypt should adopt the same rule in Article 232 of the said Code.[1]

Ancient Greeks (with the exception of the Spartans) and ancient Romans

[1] Sanhuri, *Masadir al-haqq*, Vol. III, p. 194.

used to charge heavy interest, with the peculiarity that capital and interest were secured by the person of the debtor, which meant that if such a debtor was unable to repay what was due he had to become the creditor's slave. The Athenian reformer, Solon (640–560 B.C.), achieved the task that was entrusted to him of terminating civil strife in Athens by, among other measures, the cancellation of existing debts and securities and the forbidding of any future borrowing on personal security. It is also reported that, for a certain time, Solon limited the rate of interest to 12%. In Rome, slavery for debt existed till the fourth century B.C. Before that the Twelve Tables (451–450 B.C.) limited the interest rate, probably to 12%, until at the time of the Emperor Justinian (483–565 A.D.) the rate came to vary between 4% and 12% depending on the nature of the operation involved and the rank of the borrower.[2]

Jews are prohibited by their religious law from charging their co-religionists interest (Exodus XXII:25; Leviticus XXV:36, 37). This prohibition does not apply to transactions with adherents of other religions.

As for Christians, the matter of usurious interest was dealt with by the Church, for the Gospels do not contain condemnation of the charging of interest at market rate; on the contrary, the parable of the talents told by Christ seems to consider interest generated by deposits in banks not only a normal practice but even a commendable one (Matthew XXV:14–30; Luke XIX: 11–27). However, the justification for condemning the charging of interest was seen in the following saying of Christ: "And if ye lend to them of whom you hope to receive, what thank have ye? For sinners also lend to sinners, to receive as much again. But love ye your enemies, and do good, and lend, expecting nothing in return; and your reward shall be great, and ye shall be the children of the Highest: for he is kind to the ungrateful and to the selfish" (Luke VI:34–5).

The First Council of Nicaea (325 A.D.) prohibited usury among the clergy;[3] and later on the Church obtained a ruling from Charlemagne (742–814 A.D.) that this prohibition be extended to laymen.[4] It was only during the seventeenth century and under pressure of business exigencies that it was agreed that economic activity should be liberated from what were seen as obsolete limitations.[5]

The Quranic doctrine

At the time of Muhammad's Call (610 A.D.), the city of Mecca was involved in business and trade to no less an extent than its prosperous counterparts of

[2] Shaikh Draz, "L'usure", pp. 143–4.

[3] *The New Schaff–Herzog Encyclopaedia of Religious Knowledge*, Vol. XII, *s.v.* Nicaea Councils, 1910.

[4] Alfred Colling, *Banques et banquiers de Babylone à Wall Street*, pp. 38–9.

[5] L. Milliot, *Introduction à l'étude du droit Musulman*, pp. 647–8.

the West and the East. Meccans, as it is often said, had a real infatuation with such activities, which they performed vigorously; not only did they import, export and facilitate the transit of goods, but businessmen had one fear, that of "devouring their capital" (*akl al-amwal*),[6] which meant spending from idle principal and not from the profits generated by such principal. Because such businessmen were not prepared to leave their capital unproductive while awaiting the departure or arrival of caravans, they involved themselves in loans for interest, speculations and aleatory transactions.[7]

Against this background, which left little place for humanitarian propensities, the Quran proscribed the charging of interest for the loan of money.[8] The wording of the Quranic prohibition, as will later be seen in more detail, developed gradually: during the Meccan period there was merely a strong recommendation against taking interest. The outright condemnation came later, in Medina.

Nevertheless, the inevitable question "Why should *riba* be prohibited?" was asked. One author even refused to answer it, on the ground that it is not necessary "to put forth any intellectual arguments in support of the Quranic injunctions forbidding usury", for, as he expounded, "if Quranic theories come into conflict with the modern scientific theories, I find no reason to trouble my conscience. I firmly believe that the sciences of today may become the mythology of tomorrow and what Quran has said, we may not understand it today, but it is likely to become quite clear to us tomorrow".[9]

While the above assertions may stem from the heart of a true believer, the minds of Muslims and non-Muslims alike would certainly be more satisfied with an answer closer to our understanding. Often this answer is available, for it is legitimate to identify the occasion of a Sharia injunction, and to delineate the reasons for it, once disclosed. One great contemporary historian has written that "the ordinance against usury was, evidently, directed against Medinese Jews at a time when Muhammad surely needed financial support while they insisted on charging interest";[10] yet J. Schacht wrote in the *Encyclopaedia of Islam* (s.v. Riba) that there are suggestions that "the Muslim prohibition of *riba* owes less to conditions in Mecca than to the Prophet's closer acquaintance with Jewish doctrine and practice in Medina".

While affording all the respect due to these two outstanding scholars, and despite the fact that the Quran states that Jews defied their own prohibition

6 H. Lammens, *La Mecque à la veille de l'Hégire*, p. 27.

7 Ibid, p. 127.

8 Sunna and *ijmaʿ* enlarged considerably the ambit of this interdiction, as we will discover later.

9 Anwar Iqbal Qureshi, *Islam and the Theory of Interest*, pp. xx and 4.

10 P. Hitti, *Islam, a Way of Life*, p. 23.

of *riba* (s. iv:161), I do not think that the Quranic prohibition was directed against any particular people nor was it blindly modelled upon an already existing religious rule. The prohibition of *riba* was not particularly aimed at the Jews: for one thing, discontent with *riba* first occurred while the Prophet was still in Mecca (s. xxx:39), where Jews were very few and had no continuous business with him. The other reason is that, at least similarly to the Jews of Medina, which after all was more of an agricultural settlement than a commercial centre, the Meccans were dealing with usury in their city, which was entirely devoted to commerce.[11] The Muhajirun (Meccans who accompanied the Prophet in his exile to Medina) pursued their commercial activities in Medina, as is reported by the Companion Abu Hurayra, who answered his detractors (who were astonished by his vast knowledge of Muhammad's traditions): "I was a poor man serving the Messenger of Allah with all my heart while the Muhajirun and the Ansar [the Medinan Muslims] were busy in the market caring for their fortunes."[12] Moreover, one of the Companions, ʿAbdullah Ibn Salam, stated that *riba* was widespread throughout Medina, and that was interpreted as being the case after Muhammad's death and after the ejection of the Jews.[13] On the other hand, the Quranic prohibition of *riba* does not appear to be a simple replication of the Jewish doctrine, for it is much wider than the prohibition as taught by the latter and applies basically to trading both with Muslims and with non-Muslims. Besides, it cannot be said that the Prophet was hostile to commerce, as he himself was a businessman and some of his most eminent followers were merchants. Indeed, the Quran was very much concerned to differentiate between *riba* and lawful commercial transactions, as shown by the verse: "But God hath permitted sale and forbidden usury" (s. ii:275).

If, then, the reason for the prohibition of *riba* was neither political retaliation, nor expediency, nor a simple replication of a tenet taught by another religion, nor the result of a distaste for commerce, it was probably the outcome of a noble wish to grant protection to the weak against exploitation and at the same time to encourage investors and labourers to combine their resources in joint ventures such as *mudaraba* partnerships,[14] well known to the Prophet himself,[15] instead of having recourse to lending money for profit, which was often considered as being ruinous for the borrower, immoral for the lender and therefore unlawful under Sharia teaching.

[11] Lammens, La *Mecque*, pp. 27, 125 and 127; J. Schacht, *The Origins of Muhammadan Jurisprudence*, p. 251.

[12] Ahmad Amin, *Fajr al-Islam*, p. 219.

[13] *Fatawa al-Imam Muhammad Rashid Rida*, Vol. ii, p. 598.

[14] For the definition of *mudaraba* partnership, or commenda, see p. 103 below.

[15] It is reported that the Prophet entered more than once into commenda agreements where he acted as the agent-manager.

In sum, the prohibition of *riba* first came into being during the Meccan period but was not plainly stated till the Medinan period, when the Islamic community flourished; although this prohibition may well be to some extent in line with the teachings and tenets of other religions, this cannot have been its motivation; this is more likely to be found in more elevated spheres, as with the Quranic economic doctrine which introduced, among other principles, the rightful claim of beggars and the destitute to a share in the wealth of the rich (s. LXX:24, 25), and the protection of the weak and needy (s. II:177; s. IV:127) as well as fairness and honesty in commerce (s. XVII:35; s. VI:152; s. XXVI:181, 182, 183).

On the other hand, the prohibition of *riba* found in the Quran could have been interpreted in a restricted way. This would have avoided the conflict between precept and practice. "Why", as Maxime Rodinson wondered,[16] "did medieval Muslim society provide itself with ideological precepts that conflict with its practice?" Mr Rodinson sees the answer in the pressure put by ideologists upon political and legal practice: these ideologists approach the problem from the angle of seeking to conciliate the victims of such problems and not necessarily with a view to solving the practical difficulties.

Whatever the reason for an extensive and wide-ranging interpretation of the Quranic prohibition of *riba*, this interpretation has been followed for centuries by the consensus (*ijmaʿ*) of Muslims and has thus become a binding rule of law.[17] This consensus is over the broad interpretation of the prohibition, but it does not mean that the Islamic schools of law share the same view on *riba*; on the contrary each school and practically every scholar has an individual view, as will be seen later on in detail. This has made the *riba* issue one of the most debated in Islamic *fiqh*.[18]

If the broad interpretation of the prohibition of *riba* is to be changed, another consensus will be needed, and this explains the reluctance of Muslim authors to give a personal opinion on *riba*; what they normally do is to say that the problem of *riba* should be studied by a college of respected and right-minded scholars,[19] suggesting in this way the need for a new consensus.

2 Definitions

Some technical Arabic terms will be constantly encountered in this study of *riba*, and it will be necessary to define their meanings and to translate them into English whenever possible.

16 Maxime Rodinson, *Islam and Capitalism*, pp. 45–6.

17 The reality of this consensus is denied by few Muslim scholars, as it will be seen below (pp. 26, 27 and 30).

18 *Fiqh* is the science of Sharia.

19 Shaikh Draz, "L'usure", p. 156.

Riba

This is, of course, the chief of these terms. It is generally translated into English as "usury" or "interest" but in fact has a much broader sense under Sharia, as already suggested by its dictionary meaning, which is "increase" or "gain". *Riba*, in its Sharia context, can be defined, as generally agreed, as an unlawful gain derived from the quantitative inequality of the countervalues in any transaction purporting to effect the exchange of two or more species (*anwaʿ*, sing. *nawʿ*), which belong to the same genus (*jins*) and are governed by the same efficient cause (*ʿilla*, pl. *ʿilal*). Deferred completion of the exchange of such species, or even of species which belong to different genera but are governed by the same *ʿilla*, is also *riba*, whether or not the deferment is accompanied by an increase in any one of the exchanged countervalues.[20]

That being the case, usurious transactions were classified into two categories: (a) *riba al-fadl*, which is produced by the unlawful excess of one of the countervalues as described above, and (b) *riba al-nasi'a*, which is produced by delaying completion of the exchange of the countervalues, as also described above, with or without an increase or a profit.

Some scholars, including the Hanbali Ibn Qayyim al-Jawziyya,[21] added a third category, which they have named *riba al-jahiliyya* or pre-Islamic *riba*, often manifested by the lender asking the borrower at maturity date if he will settle the debt or increase it. Increase normally occurred by charging interest on the debt initially accrued. For the authors who advocated the classification of usurious transactions into three categories, this pre-Islamic *riba* (*riba al-jahiliyya*) was regarded as the one directly referred to in the Quran, while the other two categories, namely *riba al-fadl* and *riba al-nasi'a*, were referred to in the Prophet's Tradition (Hadith).[22]

In the course of the present study I have, accordingly, adopted the following terminology:

riba: unlawful advantage by way of excess or deferment
riba al-fadl: *riba* by way of excess of one of the exchanged countervalues
riba al-nasi'a: *riba* by way of deferment of completion of an exchange
riba al-jahiliyya: pre-Islamic *riba*
mal ribawi: property susceptible of *riba*

[20] Species, genus and *ʿilla* are defined below. "Exchange of countervalues" and "exchanged countervalues" are intended to mean, in the context of this book (unless otherwise stated), the two or more corporeal objects that the parties to a bilateral contract exchange between themselves as a result of the contract. That is (1) the subject-matter of a sale contract and (2) the price, when both are articles *in rem*.

[21] *Iʿlam al-muwaqqiʿin*, Vol. II, pp. 153ff., Ibn Qayyim did not infer from the division of *riba* into three categories all the effects which were to be deduced later on by Muhammad 'Abduh, Rashid Rida and others (see below pp. 28ff.).

[22] Sanhuri, *Masadir al-haqq*, Vol. III, pp. 217–18.

One thing to remember here is that not *all* increase, profit or gain is unlawful according to Sharia, but only *riba* as previously defined and as understood by the various schools of law. This is clearly emphasized by the Quranic verse already quoted: "But God hath permitted sale and forbidden usury" (s. II:275).

Genus and species

The prohibition of *riba* applies principally to the two precious metals (gold and silver) and four commodities (wheat, barley, dates and salt) mentioned in the Prophet's Tradition but also, by analogy (*qiyas*),[23] to all species (*anwaʿ*, sing. *nawʿ*) which are jointly governed by the same efficient cause (*ʿilla*) or belong jointly to any one of the genera (*ajnas*, sing. *jins*) to which the six articles named in the Tradition are subordinated. Genus (*jins*), in the present context, may be defined as a class of articles containing several subordinate classes or species; and species (*nawʿ*) may be defined as a group of articles, having certain common attributes or qualities, subordinated to a genus. The various Islamic schools of law and often scholars of the same school, disagree on the practical interpretation of the genera, as will later be seen in detail.

ʿIlla

This has several meanings, among which one is particularly relevant to the present study, namely to designate the underlying principle or objective of a Sharia injunction (*ʿillat al-hukm*). In the context of analogy (*qiyas*), which will be seen to play a decisive part in widening the *riba* prohibition (see p. 34 below), a common *ʿilla* should connect together the two elements of the analogy, namely the object of the analogy and its subject, in order to produce the analogical reasoning. The following example will throw more light on this method of legal reasoning: drinking wine (*khamr*) is forbidden by Quranic injunctions; the drinking prohibition was extended to all kinds of alcoholic drink (*nabidh*) apparently by a hadith but also by analogy, because of the common *ʿilla* of wine and alcoholic drink, which is the capacity to produce intoxication. "Efficient cause" is possibly the nearest English translation for *ʿilla* (pl. *ʿilal*); but since there is no entirely satisfactory English equivalent I shall henceforth use the Arabic term.

It is generally agreed that analogical reasoning is valid when the following conditions are met:[24]

[23] Analogy or *qiyas*, is a process of deduction by which a rule of law is applied to cases which, although not expressly, are by implication governed by a legal text, on the basis of a common efficient cause (*ʿilla*).

[24] S. Mahmasani, *Falsafat al-tashriʿ fi 'l-Islam*, p. 186.

(a) The ʿ*illa* should represent the compelling factor which has motivated or is intended by the legal rule; it should be plain and consistent.
(b) The same ʿ*illa* should appear in both elements of the analogy, object as well as subject. A mere resemblance between attributes is not sufficient.
(c) The legal rule governing the object of the analogy should be of general application and not restricted to a specific case.

3 Various interpretations of ʿ*illa* and genus

ʿ*Illa*

Zahiris.[25] The Zahiris, as a result of their dogmatic rejection of analogy (*qiyas*) as a way of determining the law, assume that the prohibition of *riba* applies solely to the six articles quoted in the hadith (gold, silver, wheat, barley, dates and salt) and cannot be extended by way of analogy to other articles. In this particular case, the Zahiri school seems less strict than the other schools, but this is only incidental; generally speaking, it was much more strict, for it applied an abstract principle without regard to the consequences.[26]

Hanafis. For the Hanafis, ʿ*illa* has two aspects: the fact that the exchanged articles belong to the same genus, and also the fact that the said articles are weighed or measured when they change hands.[27]

Shafiis consider that the ʿ*illa* for gold and silver is their property of being currency (*thamaniyya*) and for wheat, barley, dates and salt their property of being foodstuffs, which is understood by the Shafiis to be all kinds of food used to sustain the body whether as principal nourishment, spices, fruit or medicine.[28] Contrary to the Hanafi view, the Shafiis consider that the fact that the exchanged articles belong to the same genus is a requisite for the *riba* prohibition and not an element of the ʿ*illa*.[29]

Hanbalis. Ibn Qudama in his famous treatise *al-Mughni*[30] quotes three different versions relating to ʿ*illa* attributed to Ahmad Ibn Hanbal:

(a) On the authority of the first version, the ʿ*illa* for gold and silver is twofold: the exchanged articles belong to the same genus and they change hands by way of weight. As for the other four articles quoted in the hadith (wheat, barley, dates

25 Zahiris form a school of law which derives the law only from the literal text of the Quran or Sunna.
26 J. Schacht, "The schools of law", in M. Khaddouri and H. J. Liebesny (eds.), *Law in the Middle East*, Vol. I, pp. 167–8.
27 al-Sarakhsi, *al-Mabsut*, Vol. XII, pp. 116–20.
28 al-Nawawi, *Minhaj al-talibin*, trans. by L. W. C. Van Berg, Vol. I, p. 355.
29 al-Sarakhsi, *al-Mabsut*, Vol. XII, pp. 116–20.
30 Ibn Qudama, *al-Mughni*, Vol. IV, pp. 5–9.

and salt) the *ʿilla* is again twofold: the exchanged articles belong to the same genus and they change hand by way of measure (we recall that this is the Hanafi view also).

(b) According to the second version, which is close to the Shafii and Maliki ones, the *ʿilla* for gold and silver is their property of being currency (*thamaniyya*) and for the remaining four articles their property of being foodstuffs (*tuʿam*). This opinion is favoured by Ibn Qayyim al-Jawziyya.

(c) As for the third version, it says that the *ʿilla* for the four commodities quoted in the hadith is their quality of being foodstuffs which are weighable or measurable; thus there is no *riba* when the exchanged foodstuffs are neither measurable nor weighable, as in the case of exchanging apples for pomegranates (which are sold by number and not by weight); or when the exchanged countervalues are not foodstuffs, such as exchanging iron for lead. Furthermore foodstuffs, in Ibn Qudama's view, are anything that can be eaten or drunk for nourishment such as rice, corn, grains, milk and meat, or for enjoyment such as fruit, or for medication; all these articles are the same as far as *riba* is concerned.

Malikis. For the Malikis the *ʿilla* for gold and silver is their property of being currency (*thamaniyya*), as for the Shafiis; for the remaining four articles it is their property of being nourishment for mankind (or a necessary spice), provided that they can be stored for a reasonable time without perishing.[31]

Ibadis have different interpretations of *ʿilla*. Some scholars perceive that *ʿilla* is the property of the six articles mentioned in the hadith of being weighable or measurable.[32] This is close to the Hanafi view on *ʿilla*. Al-Shammakhi shares the Shafii view on the *ʿilla*, with the slight difference that instead of talking of foodstuffs, he uses the term "what is produced by the soil" (*ma anbatathu al-ard*);[33] al-Salimi did not commit himself to one view or the other but surveyed all the opinions on *ʿilla* without showing a preference. However, it will be seen later on that, as a matter of practice, this disparity in defining *ʿilla* had no great significance under Ibadi *fiqh*, for the reason that the application of the *riba* prohibition is rather limited under that *fiqh*.

Genus

Hanafis. For the Hanafis two species are deemed to belong to one genus if they bear the same name, if they are of the same origin and have the same specific use. The use that is taken into consideration should be specific and not general; thus "nourishment" considered as a whole is not a valid criterion, but the specific use of the species in question is; for example, meat and fat are considered by the Hanafis to be of different genera because they have different names and different uses. The vinegar derived from dates and

31 Ibn Juzay, *Qawanin al-ahkam al Sharʿiyya*, pp. 279–80.
32 al-Basyani, *Mukhtasar al-Basyawi*, p. 177.
33 al-Shammakhi, *al-Idah*, Vol. III, p. 28.

the vinegar derived from grapes are two genera, for they have different origins.

All varieties and kinds of dates are deemed one genus and all varieties and kinds of meats of the same breed (for example, all lamb meat or all goat meat or all camel meat) are deemed one genus, and so on; when two meats are of different genera (e.g. camel meat and goat meat), one can be sold for another with an increase provided the sale takes place in a hand-to-hand transaction and not a deferred one, for the reason that if one element of the Hanafi ʿ*illa* is met, namely the property of the two meats of being weighable, the other element, which is the singleness of the genus, is not.[34]

Shafiis consider that flours produced from different products of the soil, e.g. wheat and barley, are different genera even when they bear the same name. So it is for milks, vinegars, fats and meats; when two milks, two fats or two meats derive from two different animals, or when two vinegars derive from different fruit, they are considered two genera;[35] thus lamb fat can be exchanged for beef fat with an increase provided it is in a hand-to-hand transaction, for they are two distinct genera.[36] Furthermore, use is also taken into consideration: for example, different parts of a given animal are considered as different genera (e.g. fat and meat)[37] when they are needed for different uses.

Hanbalis. For the author of *al-Mughni*,[38] when the two different species are identified by the same name (e.g. *tamr*,"dates") and are of one origin they are subordinated to one genus; thus all dates are of the same genus even though they may be of different species. One species may be considered as a genus with respect to the category below and a species with respect to the category above. But when the two species, even though identified by the same name, are of different origins, they are considered as two genera; such is the case for vinegar derived from dates and vinegar derived from grapes, which are two genera, or flour extracted from corn and flour extracted from barley, which again are two genera. Always, according to Ibn Qudama, when two species are of the same origin, they are deemed subordinated to the same genus even though the purpose of one differs from the purpose of the other, e.g. fats perfumed with rose, or violet or jasmine are deemed of one genus when all the fats which have been used come from the same species.

Finally, one article may be formed from two genera; such are dates, which are composed of stones and edible substance, or milk, which consists of fat

34 al-Kasani, *Bada'iʿ al-sana'iʿ fi tartib al-shara'iʿ*, Vol. v, pp. 188ff.

35 al-Nawawi, *Minhaj al-talibin*, transl. by E. C. Howard, p. 125; Muhammad Ibn Muhammad, *al-Wajiz fi madhhab al-Imam al-Shafiʿi*, p. 137.

36 al-Haythami, *al-Fatawa al-kubra*, Vol. ii, p. 239.

37 Muhammad Ibn Muhammad, *al-Wajiz*, p. 138.

38 Ibn Qudama, *al-Mughni*, Vol. iv, pp. 24–5.

and milk solids; as long as the two substances are normally combined they constitute one genus, but if one substance becomes distinct from the other, then they count as two different genera.

Malikis. For the Malikis, the closeness of the purpose of two species makes them of one genus, even though the names or the origins of said species are different. Therefore lead and zinc, which are of different origins, cannot be exchanged with deferment unless it is the same quantity for the same quantity.[39] For the Malikis wheat, barley and rye are one genus; maize, millet and rice are one genus; all pulses such as beans and lentils are one genus owing to the closeness of their use.[40] Accordingly, a quantitative inequality in the exchange of wheat for barley is unlawful.[41]

Meats are three genera for the Malikis: meats of all quadrupeds are one genus, meats of all winged animals are another genus and meats of all fishes are a third genus.[42]

The grinding of wheat, the kneading of flour, the boiling of cereals, the grilling of meat do not change the origin of these articles; and extracting fat from milk does not make this milk different from the one which has retained the fat.[43]

Ibadis. Most Ibadi authors, among them al-Shammakhi,[44] give to genus a narrow meaning. For these authors the six articles mentioned in the hadith form six different genera, otherwise (they maintain) the Prophet would not have bothered to quote all the six articles. The result is that the prohibition of *riba* is often limited for those Ibadis to the unbalanced exchange of the same species; that species being susceptible of *riba*, unless the transaction takes place forthwith and there is no deferment.[45] However, even when the species susceptible of *riba* are processed and their names changed, still no deferred exchange can take place with gain, for the reason that their utility is still the same; thus no such exchange can take place between wheat and bread or milk and cheese or olives and oil, etc., while the sale of *qasl* (husks) of wheat or barley is lawful for the reason that the utility is different.[46]

Finally, if a door is sold for a measure of iron and the door contains iron nails the sale is still lawful, because the object of the transaction is the door and not the nails.[47]

39 Malik Ibn Anas, *al-Muwatta'*, pp. 549–52.
40 al-Dardir, *al-Sharh al-saghir 'ala aqrab al-masalik ila madhhab al-Imam Malik*, Vol. III, p. 74.
41 Ibid.
42 Ibn Juzay, *Qawanin*, p. 279.
43 al-Dardir, *al-Sharh*, vol III, pp. 81–2.
44 al-Shammakhi, *al-Idah*, Vol. III, p. 31.
45 Ibid., p. 32.
46 Ibid., p. 33.
47 Ibid., pp. 33–4.

4 Traditional views on *riba*

Hanafis

***Riba al-fadl* or *riba* by way of excess.** For the Hanafis this type of *riba* arises when, in a hand-to-hand transaction involving an excess in one of the countervalues, the two elements of the Hanafi *ʿilla* are met, namely the exchanged countervalues belong to the same genus and they have the property of being weighable or measurable when they change hands. The exchanged articles need not be *identical* as far as quality is concerned, otherwise the exchange of articles of the same genus, quantity and quality would not be practicable.[48] This does not mean that the quality of the exchanged countervalues is necessarily to be disregarded but merely that, if the contracting parties intend to have a close regard to quality, they will have to resort to money assessment: this means that instead of one species being exchanged for another immediately, one species is sold and then, with more or less the sale's proceeds, the required species is bought.[49]

This recourse to sale,[50] which is the only way of guaranteeing that both articles are fairly valued by money standard, is based on a hadith which says in substance that Bilal[51] came one day to the Prophet with a measure of dates of superior quality; the Prophet enquired, "From where did you bring this?" Bilal said: "We had dates of inferior quality, so I have given two measures of those dates against one measure of superior quality dates." On hearing his explanation the Prophet exclaimed: "This is clear *riba*! Do not do it again; rather, when you wish to acquire dates of superior quality first sell the dates of inferior quality and then with the sale's proceeds purchase the superior quality dates you want."[52]

***Riba al-nasiʾa* or *riba* by way of deferment.** For the Hanafis a deferred transaction gives rise to such *riba* if and when one of the two elements of their *ʿilla* is involved, i.e. when articles *either* of the same genus *or* with the property of being both weighable or both measurable when they change hands are exchanged with deferment, whether or not there is an excess in

[48] Sanhuri, *Masadir al-haqq*, Vol. III, p. 187.

[49] Shaikh Draz, "L'usure", p. 152; Ibn Qayyim al-Jawziyya *Iʿlam al-muwaqqiʿin*, Vol. II, p. 162.

[50] This sale is a genuine one and is different from sales that are used as a legal device (*hīla*) in order to overturn *riba* prohibition.

[51] A slave of Abyssinian origin who was early attracted by Muhammad's teaching, joined his little band of followers and became the first caller for prayer (*muezzin*) after being freed by Abu Bakr. Other hadiths mention the Prophet's interlocutor as being a man from Khaybar and not Bilal.

[52] This way of assessing quality in that sort of transaction is generally promoted by all Islamic schools.

one of the countervalues (if *both* elements of the Hanafi *ʿilla* are met, not only *riba al-nasiʾa* is forbidden but also *riba al-fadl*); this is demonstrated by the fact that, when properties susceptible of *riba* are involved, transactions cannot be deferred, even with no gain or benefit.

If theory can be summed up in a relatively understandable way, actual practice still leads to great confusion among experts and laymen alike. Therefore I have decided that the best way to simplify the matter is to outline in synopses the views of the different schools of law on *riba*. These synopses show the essence of the teaching of the different schools of law, with the important comment that this essence is not necessarily shared by all scholars of one school.

The Hanafi synopsis is as follows:

(a)	The exchanged countervalues are all measurable or all weighable and belong to the same genus, as the sale of wheat for wheat.	No gain permitted in a hand-to-hand transaction and no deferred transaction, even without gain.
(b)	The exchanged countervalues are all measurable or all weighable but belong to different genera, such as the sale of gold for silver.	No deferred transaction permitted, even without gain. Increase permissible in a hand-to-hand transaction.
(c)	The exchanged countervalues are none of them measurable or weighable but belong to the same genus, such as the sale of an animal for an animal.	No deferred transaction permitted, even without gain. Gain permissible in a hand-to-hand transaction.
(d)	One of the exchanged countervalues is measurable while the other is not (whether weighable or not), such as the sale of wheat for silver or pomegranates, *or*	Gain permissible whether in a hand-to-hand transaction or in a deferred one.
(e)	One of the exchanged countervalues is weighable while the other is not (whether measurable or not), such as the sale of gold for wheat or quinces.	
(f)	The exchanged countervalues are none of them measurable or weighable, and furthermore belong to different genera, such as the sale of pomegranates for quinces.	Gain permissible whether in a hand-to-hand transaction or in a deferred one.

The rules contained in (a) and (b) above lead logically to an unacceptable result: a sale of iron, copper, sugar or cotton for a deferred payment of gold or silver, and in general the sale of weighable articles with deferred payment or delivery, would be deemed unlawful, because gold and silver are weighable too. The result would be highly impractical and furthermore would render *bayʿ salam*,[53] which was performed by the Prophet himself, unlawful. Therefore, Hanafis divided weighable articles into two different categories: (1) money, namely gold and silver, weighable with a highly precise scale and (2) all other weighable articles, whose weight is determined by a normal scale. The two categories are not deemed connected by the same weighable quality, and as a consequence the sale of a weighable article for a deferred payment can be lawful.[54]

Shafiis

***Riba al-fadl* or *riba* by way of excess.** The Shafiis see this type of *riba* as occurring when, in a hand-to-hand transaction which involves an excess in one of the countervalues, their *ʿilla* – that is, their being currency or their being foodstuffs – and their requisite for the purposes of *riba* – that is, their being species subordinated to the same genus – are both present.

If foodstuffs are sold for foodstuffs of the same genus, whether weighable or not and whether measurable or not, such as the sale of wheat for wheat, or fat for fat, or water-melon for water-melon, the exchanged quantities should be equal and the transaction should be completed forthwith, otherwise the sale is void. If currency is sold for currency (exchange) and the exchanged currencies are of the same genus, such as gold for gold, or silver for silver, the two quantities should be equal and the transaction performed without deferment, otherwise the transaction is void.[55]

***Riba al-nasiʾa* or *riba* by way of deferment.** There is such a *riba* for the Shafiis when the exchange of countervalues which are all foodstuffs or all currencies, whether or not they belong to the same genus, is delayed. Thus a deferred exchange of dates for dates, or dates for wheat, or gold for gold, or gold for silver, is unlawful whether or not accompanied by an increase or profit. According to the Maliki author, Ibn Rushd, Shafiis disallow *riba* in a deferred transaction only when the exchanged countervalues belong to property susceptible of *riba* i.e. currencies or foodstuffs.[56]

The Shafiis' synopsis, therefore, is as follows:

(a)	The exchanged countervalues are all currencies or all foodstuffs and belong to the same genus, such as the sale of dates for dates or gold for gold.	No gain permitted in a hand-to-hand transaction and no deferred transaction permitted, even without gain.

[53] *Bayʿ salam* is a sale with advance payment for future delivery; for more details see below pp. 71ff.

[54] Sanhuri, *Masadir al-haqq*, Vol. III, p. 190.

[55] Ibid., pp. 187–8.

[56] Ibn Rushd, *Bidayat al-mujtahid wa nihayat al-muqtasid*, Vol. II, p. 130.

(b)	The exchanged countervalues are all currencies or all foodstuffs but belong to different genera, such as the sale of gold for silver or dates for wheat.	No deferred transaction permitted even without gain. Gain permissible in a hand-to-hand transaction.
(c)	One of the exchanged countervalues is foodstuffs, the other is not, such as the sale of wheat for iron.	No deferred transaction permitted even without gain. Gain permissible in a hand-to-hand transaction.
(d)	The exchanged countervalues are neither foodstuffs nor currencies, whether or not they belong to the same genus,[57] such as the sale of lime for lime or lime for lead.	Gain permissible whether in a hand-to-hand transaction or in a deferred one.
(e)	One of the exchanged countervalues is currency, the other is not, whether or not foodstuffs; examples are the sale of rice for silver or iron for gold.	Gain permissible whether in a hand-to-hand transaction or in a deferred one.

Hanbalis

***Riba al-fadl* or *riba* by way of excess.** Hanbali teaching with regard to this type of *riba* is summed up by Ibn Qudama[58] as follows:

(a) Articles which have, at the same time, the capacity of being measurable or weighable and the quality of being foodstuffs (*tuʿam*) such as grains, rice, vinegar and meat, are susceptible of *riba al-fadl*.

(b) Correlatively, articles which are neither measurable nor weighable and furthermore which are not foodstuffs are not susceptible of *riba al-fadl*.

(c) Articles of the same genus which are foodstuffs but not weighable or measurable and articles of the same genus which are weighable or measurable but not foodstuffs constitute a disputed issue. Ibn Qudama is of the opinion that these articles are not susceptible of *riba al-fadl*, for there is no indication of their prohibition.

Hanbalis make no distinction, as to the applicability of *riba al-fadl*, between foodstuffs for nourishment, medicine or enjoyment. Furthermore all meats and all game come under the same rule governing *riba al-fadl*. Contrary to the Hanafis, the Hanbalis consider that the prohibition of *riba* still applies when the quantity involved is negligible.[59]

Articles which are measurable or weighable but become otherwise by man's industry, as for example material in relation to clothes, are no longer

[57] al-Sarakhsi, *al-Mabsut*, Vol. XII, p. 122. The Hanafis, on the other hand, consider that, when the exchanged countervalues belong to the same genus, no gain is lawful in a deferred transaction.

[58] Ibn Qudama, *al-Mughni*, Vol. IV, p. 8.

[59] Ibid., pp. 9–10.

susceptible of *riba*.[60] Good quality and bad quality are not taken into consideration, only the equality of the countervalues, which is determined by way of measure or weight. However, if an artisan sells one gold ring for two dinars, one dinar for the value of the gold and one dinar for his skill, that is lawful.[61]

***Riba al-nasi'a* or *riba* by way of deferment.** For the Hanbalis all articles susceptible of *riba al-fadl* (*riba* by way of excess) are also – and with no dissenting opinion known – susceptible of *riba al-nasi'a* (*riba* by way of deferment). Parties to a contract involving such articles cannot depart before taking possession of their respective countervalues. Articles which belong to two different genera can be exchanged with an increase but the transaction must be concluded with no deferment.[62] There is no objection to inequality between gold and silver (although their purpose is very similar) provided the exchange is immediate.[63] When two genera are susceptible of *riba* because they are governed by the same *ʿilla*, such as two articles which are measurable or weighable or two articles which are foodstuffs, those articles cannot be exchanged with deferment; there is no dissenting opinion about it, for the Prophet has said: "If the (exchanged) articles belong to different genera, the exchange is without restraint provided it takes place in a hand-to-hand transaction." Therefore it is lawful to sell wheat for barley when the two countervalues are uneven, provided that it is in a hand-to-hand transaction; but if one of two countervalues is currency and the other one goods, deferred delivery is allowed, for that is *bayʿ salam*, which is lawful.[64]

When a property susceptible of *riba* is exchanged for another property susceptible of *riba* but of a different genus, and assuming that the *ʿilla* governing the two properties is the same, the parties cannot separate without each taking possession of his countervalue. Shafiʿi is of this opinion but not Abu Hanifa.[65] When the efficient causes are different, such as the exchange of what is measurable for what is weighable (e.g. wheat for meat), the prevalent opinion is that deferment is allowed, for the causes are different.[66] When the exchanged articles are neither weighable nor measurable nor foodstuffs, Hanbalis as well as Shafiis advocate that deferment is allowed.[67]

The following synopsis sums up Hanbali teaching with regard to *riba*:

(a)	The exchanged countervalues are all measurable or all weighable and furthermore are foodstuffs, such as the sale of rice for rice, or grain for grain.	No gain permitted in a hand-to-hand transaction and no deferred transaction, even with no gain.

[60] Ibid.
[61] Ibid., pp. 10–11.
[62] Ibid., p. 11.
[63] Ibid., p. 12.
[64] Ibid.
[65] Ibid., p. 13.
[66] Ibid., pp. 13–14.
[67] Ibid., p. 14.

(b)	The exchanged countervalues are of the same genus and all food-stuffs but neither measurable nor weighable, such as the exchange of water-melons for apples, or all measurable or all weighable but not foodstuffs, such as the exchange of gold for silver.	Gain permissible in a hand-to-hand transaction but no deferred transaction permitted, even with no gain.
(c)	The exchanged countervalues belong to different genera and are properties governed by one *ʿilla*, i.e. they are all measurable or all weighable or all foodstuffs such as the sale of wheat for barley.	Gain permissible in a hand-to-hand transaction but no deferred transaction permitted, even with no gain.
(d)	One of the exchanged counter-values is currency and the other one an article susceptible of *riba*, i.e. measurable, weighable or foodstuffs.	Gain permissible in a hand-to-hand transaction and in a deferred one.
(e)	The exchanged countervalues belong to different genera and are governed by different *ʿilal*; for example, one is measurable (wheat), and the other is weigh-able (meat).	Gain permissible in a hand-to-hand transaction and conflicting opinion regarding deferment, with a trend towards permission.
(f)	The exchanged countervalues are all neither measurable nor weigh-able nor foodstuffs; an example is the sale of riding animals.	Gain permissible whether in a hand-to-hand transaction or in a deferred one.

Malikis

***Riba al-fadl* or *riba* by way of excess.** Two conditions are necessary for the existence of such *riba*: the exchanged countervalues should belong to the same genus and should be governed by the same *ʿilla*, which is dual for the Malikis: currency (as gold and silver are defined), and nourishment for mankind which can be stored for a reasonable time without perishing (a description which covers such commodities as wheat, barley, salt, dates).[68]

If the exchanged countervalues are currencies of the same genus (gold for gold or silver for silver), no increase is lawful in a hand-to-hand transaction (nor in a deferred one); on the contrary, if the exchanged currencies are of different genera (gold for silver), increase in a hand-to-hand transaction is lawful; however the transaction, even with no gain, cannot be deferred but should be performed immediately.[69]

68 al-Dardir, *al-Sharh*, p. 73.

69 Ibn Juzay, *Qawanin*, pp. 275ff.

***Riba al-nasi'a* or *riba* by way of deferment.** Deferment, even with no increase or profit, is unlawful in any transaction involving the exchange of countervalues which are storable nourishment for mankind, even though the exchanged countervalues belong to different genera. Contrary to the view of the Shafiis, medication can be the subject of a deferred transaction, and water is a disputed issue.[70]

When the exchanged countervalues are foodstuffs but are not governed by the Maliki *'illa* (that is, of being storable nourishment for mankind), and whether or not they belong to the same genus, gain is permitted in a hand-to-hand transaction but the transaction cannot be deferred even with no gain.[71] As for currency, the exchange cannot be deferred even if it does not involve any gain[72] and exchange with gain should take place forthwith, whether the currency is assessed by weight or by number.

The Maliki synopsis can be set out as follows:

(a) The exchanged countervalues are all currencies or all storable nourishment for mankind and belong to the same genus as in the exchange of dinars for dinars or wheat for wheat.	No gain permissible in a hand-to-hand transaction and no deferred transaction even with no gain.[73]
(b) The exchanged countervalues are all currencies or all storable nourishment for mankind but belong to different genera, for example the exchange of dinars for dirhams or wheat for broad beans.	No deferred transaction permitted even with no gain. Gain permissible in a hand-to-hand transaction.
(c) The exchanged countervalues are all foodstuffs which are not governed by the Maliki *'illa* whether or not they belong to the same genus,[74] such as the sale of bananas for lettuce.	No deferred transaction permitted even with no gain. Gain permissible in a hand-to-hand transaction.
(d) The exchanged countervalues are neither edible nor drinkable but are all either weighable or measurable, belong to the same genus and furthermore serve the same purpose,[75] such as the sale of material for material.	No deferred transaction permitted even with no gain. Gain permissible in a hand-to-hand transaction.

70 Ibid., p. 279.

71 Ibn Abi Zayd al-Qayrawani, *al-Risala, ou Traîté abrégé de droit Malékite et morale Musulmane*, p. 138; Ibn Juzay, *Qawanin*, p. 279.

72 Ibid., p. 275.

73 al-Dardir, *al-Sharh*, p. 47.

74 That they are foodstuffs is sufficient for disallowing deferment. Ibn Rushd, *Bidayat al-mujtahid*, Vol. II, p. 129.

75 Malik Ibn Anas, *al-Muwatta'*, p. 552; Ibn Rushd, *Bidayat al-mujtahid*, Vol. II, pp. 132–3.

(e)	The exchanged countervalues are not foodstuffs and do not belong to the same genus such as the sale of material for currency.	Gain permissible whether in a hand-to-hand transaction or in a deferred one.

Ibadis

The Ibadis have a comparatively lenient view on *riba*: for them there is *riba* only if all of these three requisites are met: (1) the exchanged articles are subordinated to the same genus; (2) there is an excess in one of the countervalues and (3) there is deferment.[76] In other words, Ibadis forbid *riba* only in deferred transactions involving the exchange of unequal quantitative countervalues subordinated to the same genus.

The Ibạdi synopsis is as follows:

(a)	The exchanged countervalues are governed by the same *ʿilla* and belong to the same genus which is restrictively interpreted by this *fiqh* (p. 18 above).	No gain permitted in a deferred transaction. Gain permissible in a hand-to-hand transaction.
(b)	The exchanged countervalues belong to two different genera, whether or not they are governed by the same *ʿilla*.	Gain permissible both in a hand-to-hand transaction and in a deferred one.

5 Other views on *riba*

There is no doubt that the majority of Muslim scholars and learned men have interpreted and continue to place a wide-ranging interpretation on the prohibition of *riba*; a few of them have endeavoured to confine such prohibition within more restricted limits. But because these few are to be found among the most eminent, their views carry some weight and deserve to be reported. I have therefore in the following subsections given summaries of some independent views on *riba* which are deemed most representative. Needless to say, each of these views has been the subject of incessant discussion – not reported here, in an attempt to avoid further complicating a question which is already complex.

Ibn ʿAbbas

ʿAbdullah Ibn ʿAbbas was a cousin of the Prophet and was born two years before the Hijra (622 A.D.). He is better known for his vast knowledge of Tradition than for the controversial political role that he played after the Prophet's death.

[76] al-Shammakhi, *al-Idah*, Vol. III, p. 24; al-Basyani, *Mukhtasar*, p. 176.

Ibn ʿAbbas, as he is habitually called, as well as some of the Prophet's Companions,[77] considered that the only unlawful *riba* is *riba al-jahiliyya* (pre-Islamic *riba*) manifested, as we have already seen (p. 13 above), by the lender asking the borrower at maturity date: "Will you settle the debt or increase it?" Increase normally occurred by charging interest accrued on the interest already accounted by the time the loan agreement was concluded. On the contrary, *riba al-nasi'a* and *riba al-fadl*, both provided for in the famous hadith in relation to the six articles, gold, silver, wheat, barley, dates and salt, are lawful.

This liberal interpretation of *riba* relies on a hadith that Ibn ʿAbbas has himself reported and which, in his opinion, has superseded the previous one. This last hadith on *riba*, the authenticity of which is not generally denied but which is interpreted in conflicting ways, says in substance: "No *riba* except in the *nasi'a*" (*nasi'a* here is understood as being the pre-Islamic *riba*). The opponents of Ibn ʿAbbas' interpretation of this hadith see it as putting more emphasis on *riba al-nasi'a* and not as superseding the previous hadiths.

Ibn Qayyim

Ibn Qayyim al-Jawziyya (1292/1350 A.D.) was a Hanbali theologian and a disciple of the celebrated Ibn Taymiyya. He, as early as the fourteenth century, taught legal concepts which were to be rediscovered centuries after his time.[78]

In one of his treatises,[79] Ibn Qayyim differentiates between "hidden *riba*" (*riba khafi*) and "manifest riba" (*riba jali*). Manifest *riba* is *riba* by way of deferment (*riba al-nasi'a*) and hidden *riba* is *riba* by way of increase (*riba al-fadl*). Hidden *riba* is not forbidden in itself but only when it is a way to gain manifest *riba*, which *is* forbidden for itself. Because of such a distinction, Ibn Qayyim saw that the degree of prohibition was not the same in both categories: it was much stronger in manifest *riba* or *riba al-nasi'a* than in hidden *riba* or *riba al-fadl*. As a consequence, manifest *riba* (*riba al-nasi'a*) cannot become lawful except in the case of pressing necessity (*darura mulji'a*), like that which allows the eating of carrion. On the contrary, hidden *riba* (*riba al-fadl*) can become lawful in case of need (*haja*) only, which is obviously governed by less stringent conditions than "pressing necessity".[80] In other words, *riba al-fadl* or hidden *riba* is a "grey area": it is prohibited when there is a fear that it may be used to attain *riba al-nasi'a*, and it is allowed in case of pressing need.

77 Usama Ibn Zayd, ʿAbdullah Ibn Masʿud, ʿUrwa Ibn Zubayr, Zayd Ibn Arqam and leading Meccan scholars.

78 N. Saleh, *The General Principles of Saudi Arabian and Omani Company Laws*, p. 19.

79 *Iʿlam al-muwaqqiʿin*, Vol. II, pp. 154ff.

80 Sanhuri, *Masadir al-haqq*, Vol. III, p. 206.

ʿAbduh and Rida

A modernist party, Salafiyya, was founded in Egypt in 1883 by the pan-Islamic forerunner Jamal al-Din al-Afghani (1839–1897) and by his most brilliant disciple Muhammad ʿAbduh (1849–1905), with the purpose of bringing about an Islamic renaissance. Muhammad ʿAbduh, who ended his life as Grand Mufti of Egypt, helped his favourite pupil Rashid Rida to establish in 1897 a monthly magazine called *al-Manar* (The Lighthouse) which was to serve as the doctrinal organ of the party. Muhammad ʿAbduh and Rashid Rida issued a vast number of *fatawa* (sing. *fatwa*: response on a point of Islamic law issued by a learned man) and inevitably had to tackle the question of *riba*. Their views on *riba* can be summarized as follows:

(a) The only disallowed *riba* is *riba al-jahiliyya* (pre-Islamic *riba*), which is the manifest (*jali*) *riba* and consequently is prohibited not as a way of performing an usurious transaction but as an usurious transaction in itself. As for the two other sorts of *riba*, namely *riba al-fadl* and *riba al-nasiʾa* (both provided for in Hadith and not in the Quran), their prohibition tends to close the loopholes which otherwise might permit manifest *riba* (*riba jali*). Thus *riba al-fadl* and *riba al-nasiʾa* are under a presumption of prohibition and this presumption is not conclusive but rebuttable. Thus again the sale of any of the six articles mentioned in the hadith, with an increase and whether in a hand-to-hand transaction or in a deferred one, is disallowed only if it is intended to lead to manifest *riba* (*riba jali*), which takes place when interest accrues on interest already accounted by the time the transaction was concluded.[81]

(b) As a result, the first increase on the termed loan is lawful, even though agreed in consideration of the delayed term of payment. But if, at maturity date, it is decided to postpone that maturity date against a further increase, that is the unlawful *riba al-nasiʾa*.[82]

(c) The consequence which comes to mind is that whereas *riba jali*, the manifest *riba*, can be deemed lawful only in case of pressing necessity, such as the one which allows the eating of carrion, the two other sorts of *riba*, namely *riba al-nasiʾa* and *riba al-fadl* (both provided for by Hadith and not by the Quran) are regarded with aversion (*karahiyya*) but not as under a rule of prohibition.[83]

(d) Finally, it is attributed to Shaikh Muhammad ʿAbduh that he found ways to show that under Islamic law both interest generated by savings bank accounts and that generated by insurance policies were admissible.

Sanhuri

ʿAbd al-Razzaq Sanhuri is a great contemporary Egyptian authority on Islamic and positive law. Although for him prohibition of *riba* is the rule and has nothing to do with aversion (*karahiyya*),[84] nevertheless the distinction

81 *Fatawa al-Imam Muhammad Rashid Rida*, Vol. II, p. 606.

82 Ibid., pp. 608–9.

83 Sanhuri, *Masadir al-haqq*, Vol. III, p. 220. *Karahiyya* is a religious censure with no practical effect on the transaction itself.

84 Sanhuri, *Masadir al-haqq*, Vol. III, pp. 222–34.

between *riba al-jahiliyya*, *riba al-fadl* and *riba al-nasi'a* should be maintained according to the following analysis: *riba al-fadl* is a way to achieve *riba al-nasi'a* which is a way to achieve *riba al-jahiliyya*; for it is sufficient, as far as *riba al-nasi'a* is concerned to allow payment to be postponed once the debt has matured, charging further interest, so as to attain *riba al-jahiliyya*. Consequently *riba al-fadl* and *riba al-nasi'a* are not under a direct prohibition (contrary to pre-Islamic *riba*, which is), but under a prohibition of illicit means – a prohibition designed to close the loopholes which might lead to pre-Islamic *riba*.[85]

The result of such degrees of prohibition is that *riba al-jahiliyya* is allowed only in case of pressing necessity (*darura mulihha*), while *riba al-fadl* and *riba al-nasi'a* are deemed lawful in case of need (*haja*).[86]

Daoualibi

Mr Daoualibi is a contemporary Syrian politician and journalist. He is well known for his lenient approach towards secular matters (*muʿamalat*), and *riba* is one of them. His view on *riba* is expressed in a lecture given in Paris in 1951[87] whereby he described the practice of credit allowed during the Prophet's time as being mainly unproductive and used as a way to take advantage of the needy;[88] this has been remedied by Islam through *zakat*,[89] *sadaqa*[90] and the contract of *mudaraba* partnership. But today things have changed: people do not borrow money for their mere subsistence but so as to make money and thereby strengthen the economy of the nation; therefore contracts of loan are now thought of as productive. Consequently, Daoualibi is of the opinion that Islam should make a distinction between productive and unproductive interest, and should allow the former.

Shaikh Draz

Shaikh Draz delivered a lecture on *riba*[91] during the Conference in which Mr Daoualibi also participated. Shaikh Draz gave a notable exposition of the problem of *riba* and of the foundation of its prohibition, ending his lecture with the inevitable question: "Is the actual economic system an exception to the prohibition of *riba*?" Shaikh Draz refused to answer that question, on the ground that the problem cannot be solved by individual opinions but should be submitted to the profound and thoughtful examination of several

85 Ibid., pp. 222–37. 86 Ibid., p. 237.

87 "La théorie de l'usure en droit Musulman", pp. 139ff.

88 This point of history is rightly disputed by Muhammad ʿAbdullah al-ʿArabi in an article published by *al-Azhar*, the magazine of the Academy of Islamic Research, issue of May 1965, pp. 83ff. (in English).

89 *Zakat* is a tax levied on the gross assets of Muslims: its payment amounts to a religious duty.

90 Voluntary alms-giving.

91 "L'usure en droit musulman", pp. 143ff.

committees gathered from various countries and with judicial, political and economic expertise.[92] He thus expressed the view that a new consensus over *riba* is needed.

Zaydan Abu al-Karim Hassan

That is not the opinion of Zaydan Abu al-Karim Hassan as expressed in a paper he has recently published in the magazine *al-Azhar*.[93] For this author there is no consensus over *riba* and there has never been one, for the Companions were never in agreement over that issue. For Zaydan the only disallowed *riba* is *riba al-jahiliyya*, the same as that condemned by Ibn ʿAbbas on account of the hadith "No *riba* except in the *nasi'a*" (understood here as being the pre-Islamic *riba*), which in his opinion has superseded the other hadiths on *riba*.

6 *Ribawi* transactions with non-Muslims

Muslim jurists divided the world into Abode of Islam (*Dar al-Islam*) and Abode of War (*Dar al-Harb*). The former comprises the countries where the ordinances of Islam are established and which are under the rule of a Muslim sovereign, whereas the latter category includes all countries which are not deemed *Dar al-Islam* and which are actually or potentially a seat of war for Muslims until they are turned by conquest into Abode of Islam.[94] Besides *Dar al-Islam* and *Dar al-Harb*, the existence of a third division is recognized by some schools of law under the name of *Dar al-Sulh* (Territories under Treaties). Countries which by agreement with Islamic countries are in a state neither of Islam nor of war form that third category.[95] On account of the numerous treaties binding modern states together, and on account of a certain habit of tolerance, *Dar al-Sulh* has taken a predominant place in the classification.

That is, of course, a simplified description of the Islamic vision of the world; nevertheless, it allows us to ask a question which relates to the subject of the present study: "Does the prohibition of *riba* apply to transactions concluded between Muslims and non-Muslims in any of *Dar al-Islam*, *Dar al-Harb* or *Dar al-Sulh*?" Before answering that question we have to bear in mind that a non-Muslim in *Dar al-Islam* is either a belligerent (*harbi*), a *dhimmi* (a non-Muslim settled in *Dar al-Islam* on payment of *jizya* or poll

92 Ibid., p. 156.

93 "Riba qabl al-Islam wa baʿduhu" (*Riba* before and after Islam), pp. 956ff. in issue no. 5, Cairo 1980.

94 Gibb and Kramers (eds.), *Shorter Encyclopaedia of Islam*, s.v. Dar al-Harb and Dar al-Islam; Majid Khaddouri, *War and Peace in the Law of Islam*, pp. 155ff., Johns Hopkins University Press, Baltimore, Md., 1955.

95 Gibb and Kramers (eds.), *Shorter Encyclopaedia of Islam*, s.v. Dar al-Sulh.

tax) or a *musta'man* (a non-Muslim who entered *Dar al-Islam* under *aman*).[96] It is highly unlikely that a non-Muslim belligerent (*harbi*) would be party to any business transaction concluded with a Muslim under normal circumstances and involving the question of *riba*. On the other hand a *dhimmi* or a *musta'man* would most probably conduct some business activity during his sojourn in *Dar al-Islam*.

The general rule under Islamic Sharia is that such a *dhimmi* or *musta'man* is under an obligation to abide by the Sharia rules and principles with regard to secular transactions as if he were a Muslim, save for some restrictions and a few exceptions such as his being permitted to deal with wine and pork.[97] In other words a *dhimmi* or a *musta'man* cannot enter a *ribawi* transaction in *Dar al-Islam*, whether with a Muslim or a non-Muslim.

Conversely, a Muslim in *Dar al-Harb* or *Dar al-Sulh* is either a belligerent or a *musta'man* – that is, a Muslim who benefits from a pledge of security while he is either in *Dar al-Harb* or in *Dar al-Sulh*. It is quite unlikely that the former would be involved in a *ribawi* transaction with a non-Muslim, whereas the latter may well conclude business transactions with non-Muslims. Could the Muslim *musta'man* be party to a *ribawi* transaction with a non-Muslim during his sojourn in a non-Muslim territory?[98]

Most Hanafi authors teach that in such a case there is no wrong if the Muslim *musta'man* takes the property of non-Muslims with their consent, by any means except for deceit. Consequently a *ribawi* transaction can be concluded between a Muslim *musta'man* or *dhimmi* and a non-Muslim outside Muslim territory.[99] The Hanafi opinion is not shared by the other schools of law whose teachings are under our scrutiny. Hanbalis, Malikis,[100] Shafiis[101] and Ibadis[102] hold that the prohibition of *riba* applies also to transactions concluded outside Muslim territory between a Muslim *musta'man* and a non-Muslim.

omche in Paki=stan

Apparently the traditional Hanafi view on this particular point has been

96 *Aman* is a pledge of security by virtue of which the *harbi* would be entitled to protection, while he is in the *Dar al-Islam*, by Muslim authority. No longer at war with Islam during his sojourn, the *harbi* would become a *musta'man* (secured). The duration of the *aman* must by necessity be less than a year for if the *harbi* requests a period which exceeded one year he must pay the poll tax and become a *dhimmi* (Khaddouri, *War and Peace*, p. 163).

97 'Abd al-Karim Zaydan, *Ahkam al-dhimmiyin wa 'l-musta'manin*, pp. 547ff.; al-Kasani, *Bada'i'*, Vol. v, p. 192 and Vol. vii, p. 132; Ibn Qudama, *al-Mughni*, Vol. v, p. 566; al-Shafi'i, *al-Umm*, Vol. iv, p. 200; al Dardir, *al-Sharh*, Vol. iv, p. 78; Atfish, *Sharh al-Nil*, Vol. viii, p. 540.

98 Two Muslims cannot lawfully perform a *ribawi* transaction while in *Dar al-Harb* or *Dar al-Sulh*.

99 al-Shaybani, *Sharh Kitab al-siyar al-kabir*, Vol. iv, pp. 1486–8; Ibn 'Abidin, *Radd al-muhtar*, Vol. v, pp. 185–6; al-Kasani, *Bada'i'*, Vol. vii, pp. 131–2.

100 Ibn Qudama, *al-Mughni*, Vol. iv, pp. 45–6; al-Khiraqi, *Mukhtasar*, p. 204; Ibn al-Farra', *al-Ahkam al-sultaniyya*, p. 136, Egypt (no date).

101 al-Mawardi, *al-Ahkam al-sultaniyya*, p. 141.

102 al-Basyani *Mukhtasar*, p. 14.

upheld by Pakistan. There interest seems an accepted practice for transactions of foreign banks and foreign branches of Pakistani banks and also for certain transactions of Pakistani banks with foreign borrowers. The problem of avoiding the intermingling of interest and non-interest income was mainly resolved by entrusting the administration of foreign branches of Pakistani banks to a separate corporation which receives foreign currency deposit business.[103]

[103] David Suratgar, "Prospects for cooperation between Western and Islamic financial systems", a lecture delivered during a conference on Islamic Banking held on 18 September 1984. That lecture and others have been published in English under the title *Islamic Banking* by the Middle East Association and Monadnock Institute, London.

APPENDIX 1

Sources of the prohibition of *riba*

Quranic texts

Quranic direct references to *riba* are to be found in four Suras. The first Sura was revealed in Mecca and the remaining three in Medina. The relevant verses form, in some Muslim scholars' view, an ascending scale which starts with a mere judgement of value, followed by an implicit prohibition, then a limited one and finally a total and conclusive prohibition.[1]

Mention of *riba* in the Meccan Sura is, in translation, as follows:

s. xxx:39 That which ye provide with the prospect of an increase through the property of [other] people, will have no increase with God; but that which ye provide for charity, seeking the countenance of God, [will increase]: it is these who will get a recompense multiplied.

Mention of *riba* in the three Medinan Suras is, in translation, as follows:

s. iv:161 That they took usury, though they were forbidden; and that they devoured men's substance wrongfully, we have prepared for those among them who reject faith a grievous punishment.

s. iii:130 O ye who believe! devour not usury, doubled and multiplied; but fear God; that ye may [really] prosper.

s. ii:275 Those who devour usury will not stand except as stands one whom The Evil One by his touch hath driven to madness. That is because they say: "Sale is like usury", but God hath permitted sale and forbidden usury. Those who after receiving Direction from their Lord, desist, shall be pardoned for the past; their case is for God [to judge]. But those who repeat [the offence] are Companions of the Fire: they will abide therein [for ever].

s. ii:276 God will deprive usury of all blessing, but will give increase for deeds of charity: for he loveth creatures ungrateful and wicked.

s. ii:278 O ye who believe! Fear God, and give up what remains of your demand for usury, if ye are indeed believers.

s. ii:279 If ye do not respond, expect war from God and his Apostle: but if ye repent, ye shall have your capital sums: deal not unjustly, and ye shall not be dealt with unjustly.

According to Muslim scholars,[2] Verse 275 of Sura ii was revealed after the legitimacy of the prohibition of *riba* was questioned by some of the Prophet's

[1] Shaikh Draz, "L'usure", pp. 143ff.

[2] Ibid., pp. 153–4.

contemporaries, who affected not to see the difference between sale and loan, adding that if the profit generated by a loan is to be forbidden, then the profit produced by sale should also be prohibited. To this apparently naive view, the Quran had replied "God hath permitted sale and forbidden usury."

Another interesting detail found in Verse 275 of Sura II is that the Quranic revelation contrasted sale (*bay*ʿ) and *riba*; in fact, a sale contract has always been considered the typical contract in Islamic law, and the one on which nearly all other contracts are modelled; this is why one of the Quran translators[3] has, in this very context, translated *bay*ʿ as "trade".

Sunna (deeds, utterances and unspoken approvals of the Prophet)

The Quranic prohibition of *riba* is limited to loan agreements, but soon it was to be extended by several hadiths to the exchange of currencies and denominated articles, which became property susceptible of *riba* (*mal ribawi*). These hadiths are reported in numerous accounts with slight differences, the one reproduced hereafter is representative of the rule that the Prophet intended to convey although it has a concise form:

[Exchange] gold for gold, silver for silver, wheat for wheat, barley for barley, dates for dates, salt for salt, measure for measure and hand-to-hand. If the [exchanged] articles belong to different genera, the exchange is without restraint provided it takes place in a hand-to-hand transaction.

***Fiqh* (jurisprudence)**

Although the Sunna prohibition of *riba* generally refers to barter, it was understood from the outset to comprise sale transactions; not just for the reason that barter is a kind of sale (Article 122 of the Majalla, the Ottoman Civil Code based on Sharia),[4] but also because in the Prophet's time sale transactions continued to be performed by exchanging articles *in rem*, currency being scarce. Even in a commercial city like Mecca, currencies were not in abundance; as a substitute, recourse was made to precious metals, bullion or powder of gold and silver which passed by weight;[5] and exchange was still very popular. Furthermore, the trend of doctrine towards rigour as far as *riba* is concerned, and also the need for submitting all secular transactions to the same rule, have had the effect of making the *riba* prohibition apply not only to contracts of loan (as stipulated in the Quran) and contracts of barter or sale as in the Sunna, but to all sorts of transactions involving the exchange of countervalues.[6]

But if nearly all schools of law were in agreement in extending the prohibition of *riba* to all sorts of transactions which involve the exchange of countervalues, and if nearly all schools of law, except the Zahiri one, widened the prohibition of *riba* beyond the six articles mentioned in the hadith (gold, silver, wheat, barley, dates and salt), on the ground of analogy, yet they often dissented when it came to the practical interpretation of this hadith. Their dissensions stemmed on the whole from their different views on *ʿilla*, which is the core of the method of reasoning called analogy (*qiyas*); and to make the issue more complicated, genus, considered by the Hanafis as merely one element of the *ʿilla* and by the Shafiis as a requisite was also diversely understood and construed. (The main interpretations of *ʿilla* and genus are examined in Section 3 above.)

[3] Quran; translation by ʿAbdullah Yusuf ʿAli, note 326 under s. II: 275.
[4] S. Mahmasani, *al-Awzaʿi*, p. 301.
[5] Lammens, *La Mecque*, pp. 124–8.
[6] S. Mahmasani, *al-Awzaʿi*, pp. 298–9.

CHAPTER 2

Qard (loan of fungible commodities)

1 *Qard* and *riba*

Generally speaking, positive law[1] describes loan as a contract whereby one party lends another a property for some time. When the lent property is a non-fungible article, only the right of use is transferred to the borrower who, on maturity date or on demand, as the case may be, must restore it in as good condition as he took it, fair wear and tear excepted. This loan of a non-fungible article is called a "proper loan" (the "Commodatum" of Roman law). On the other hand, when the lent property is a fungible commodity, ownership is transferred to the borrower, who may consume or use it up, but must on maturity date or on demand, as the case may be, restore an equal amount of the borrowed commodity and it must be of the same quality. This latter loan is called "improper loan" (the "Mutuum" of Roman law).

In the same manner, Sharia distinguishes between two types of loan: one is the *ʿariya*, a loan *for use*, which transfers the usufruct of a property, temporarily and gratuitously, to the borrower, while ownership of the loaned object remains with the lender. Either the lender or the borrower may rescind the contract at will and terminate the loan. But as long as the *ʿariya* is in effect, its object is held on trust by the borrower who, in the eyes of the Hanafis and Malikis, is not liable for its destruction, loss or diminution in value unless caused by his fault or negligence. On the other hand, Hanbalis and Shafiis consider that the borrower *is* liable for such hazards, whether or not he was at fault or negligent.[2]

The second type of loan recognized by Sharia is the *qard*, which "involves the loan of fungible commodities: that is, goods which may be estimated and replaced according to weight, measure or number. In this case the borrower undertakes to return the equivalent or likes of that he has received but without any premium on the property, which would, of course, be construed

1 Positive law is the law given by persons of authority, as distinct from moral or sacred law given by God or with God's guidance. It refers also to Western laws and to the secular statutes borrowed therefrom by Islamic countries.

2 S. Mahmasani, "Transactions in the Shariʿa", in Khaddouri and Liebesny (eds.), *Law in the Middle East*, Vol. I, p. 133; S. Mahmasani, *al-Awzaʿi*, p. 333.

as interest. The most likely object of a *qard* loan would be currency or other standard means of exchange."[3]

The present chapter is solely concerned with *qard*, and that raises a question which is a natural extension of the *riba* problem dealt with above: "Does Sharia deem *qard* a *ribawi* contract i.e. a contract under a conclusive presumption of *riba*?" This question, as Sanhuri commented, seems surprising at first, for in the eyes of positive law a loan contract is the first among *ribawi* transactions. That is not the case under Sharia, which regards a loan contract as basically a gratuitous transaction, and that by itself negates the existence of *riba*; nevertheless a loan contract does become a *ribawi* transaction, by analogy with sale, when it secures to the lender an interest or a premium.[4]

Because *qard* is not basically a *ribawi* transaction but is treated as such by analogy, most schools of law teach that when the borrower gives back willingly more or better than he has borrowed, that is lawful, provided that the increase (in the quantity or in the quality) was not a *requisite* of the *qard*.[5] Furthermore resorting to *hila*, with intent to overturn the prohibition of agreeing beforehand on the payment of an interest or a premium, is lawful[6] at least for the Hanafis and Shafiis, the two main Islamic schools of law which allow the use of *hiyal*.[7]

Consequently, Sanhuri placed interest or premium stipulated in a *qard* in the same category as *riba al-nasi'a* and *riba al-fadl*, both forbidden, not for themselves but as a means to attain *riba al-jahiliyya*, which is prohibited for itself. The most interesting effect that Sanhuri inferred for such a distinction was that the prohibition upon agreeing on an interest or premium in the loan contract can be lifted in case of need (*haja*).[8] In an inconspicuous note appearing at the bottom of one of the pages dealing with this matter,[9] Sanhuri states that "early legal scholars described *qard* in a way which makes it more like a voluntary almsgiving, but this nature has changed nowadays and a *qard* becomes a means for providing the necessary capital for production".[10]

This view on the change in the concept of *qard* and its purpose is not accepted by all Muslim scholars; many of them deny that *qard* is now

[3] A. Udovitch, *Partnership and Profit in Medieval Islam*, p. 107.

[4] Sanhuri, *Masadir al-haqq*, Vol. III, p. 237.

[5] Ibid., p. 240.

[6] Ibid.

[7] *Hiyal* (sing. *hila*) are described as lawful means used, knowingly and voluntarily, to reach an unlawful objective.

[8] Sanhuri, *Masadir al-haqq*, Vol. III, pp. 240–1. See also pp. 28–9 above.

[9] Ibid., note 1 of p. 241.

[10] Sanhuri's view on the change which has occurred in the purpose of a loan is also shared by M. Daoualibi in his "La théorie de l'usure en droit Musulman", in *Travaux de la Semaine Internationale de Droit Musulman*, p. 141.

different from what it was during the Prophet's time and one of them[11] expressed his view as follows: "The Prophet's saying that 'every loan entailing benefit is usury' would also seem to have been forgotten. The Prophet here did not differentiate between situations where borrowed capitals had relieved borrower distress, or had been invested in some productive enterprise. Had God meant that differentiation, or known that it would be beneficial to mankind a relevant stipulation would not have been omitted from the Quran."

Contemporary Muslim authors are obviously not in agreement on the relative lawfulness on repaying a *qard* with interest or a premium added. Their disagreement is not something new. Already classical authors, adherents of different schools of law, had conflicting views on how, when and where a *qard* should be repaid. Specific studies were devoted to the return, whether in money or in kind, that a lender might or might not derive from a *qard*. It is perhaps useful to present a brief survey of the teaching of the four Sunni schools and that of the Ibadi on the repayment of a *qard*.

2 Repayment of a *qard* according to *fiqh*

What should be repaid to the lender, and where?

Hanafis teach that a *qard* entails a guarantee that the like (*al-mithl*) should be given back. Thus the subject-matter of a *qard* should have a like; such is the case with regard to commodities which are measurable or weighable or accounted by number when alike. As a result it is not allowed to lend agricultural products and articles accounted by number which have no like at the place of repayment; the reason is that neither the borrowed product nor the like can be given back.[12] When wheat (a measurable article) is borrowed, then the borrower is under the obligation to give back the like whether wheat's price has gone up or down. The same rule applies to what is weighable or accounted by number.[13] When the borrowed article is currency which has become obsolete, the borrower, according to Abu Hanifa, is liable to give back the like (obsolete currency); but Abu Yusuf and Muhammad, the two distinguished disciples of Abu Hanifa, did not share this view and taught that the value should be given back, pursuant to the rule which says that the borrower should give back the like but if that is not possible then he should give back the value.[14]

When the object of a *qard* is dirhams (silver coins) of commercial value

11 Muhammad ʿAbdullah al-ʿArabi, "Contemporary bank transactions and Islam's views thereon", in *al-Azhar* (Academy of Islamic Research), issue of May 1965, pp. 84–5.

12 al-Kasani, *Bada'iʿ*, Vol. VII, p. 395.

13 Jaziri, *al-Fiqh ʿala al-madhahib al-arbaʿa*, Vol. II, p. 339, 6th edn.

14 al-Kasani, *Bada'iʿ*, p. 395.

and the lender and borrower meet in a country where the latter has not this type of money at his disposal, although it is in circulation, then the lender has three options: to refrain from claiming his debt until the borrower returns to the place of payment (the location where the *qard* took place), or to give the borrower a respite until he goes to fetch the money and comes back (while providing a guarantor for the interim), or to take the value of the object of the *qard* if he does not want to wait any longer. That is also the case when unripe fruit (*rutb*) is the *qard*'s object: if *rutb* is out of season, then the lender has the option either to wait until it is available or to take the value forthwith. If there is no *rutb* in the country, then the lender will receive the value.[15]

Hanbalis hold the view that when the borrowed article is a fungible property, the borrower may compel the lender to take it back, whether or not its value has fluctuated, provided it has not suffered a defect.[16] When the borrowed article is a measurable or weighable property, the like (*al-mithl*) should be paid back;[17] in the event of the like not being available, the borrower is indebted to the extent of the value, whether the value has increased since the time the *qard* took place or decreased by the time the like has disappeared from the market, for the reason that the borrower is indebted under a personal obligation.[18] When the borrowed article is *mal mutaqawwam* (a corporeal or incorporeal – except for the hanafis – property with a lawful market value), such as jewellery, the lender is not compelled to take back the actual loaned article but is entitled to ask for its value.[19] This value is assessed at the time when the borrower takes possession of the lent article.[20] When the borrowed articles are token coins (*fulus*, sing. *fals*) or broken dirhams (*mukassarat*) which have been banned by order of the authorities, the lender is entitled to their value and is not compelled to take them back, for they are deemed to have suffered a defect while in the borrower's possession; furthermore they constitute less than the lender's right.[21]

The value of obsolete currency should be assessed at the time the borrower takes it, whether the value has depreciated a little or greatly;[22] the value should be assessed in a currency different from the one which was originally the object of the *qard*.[23] According to Ibn Qudama,[24] Malik,

[15] Ibid.

[16] al-Bahuti, *al-Rawd al-murbi'*, Vol. II, p. 190, 6th edn.; al-Ba'li, *al-Rawd al-nadi*, p. 233; Ibn Qudama, *al-Mughni*, Vol. IV, p. 360.

[17] Ibn Qudama, *al-Mughni*, Vol. IV, p. 352.

[18] al-Ba'li, *al-Rawd al-nadi*, p. 233.

[19] al-Bahuti, *al-Rawd al-murbi'*, Vol. II, p. 190.

[20] Ibid., and al-Ba'li, *al-Rawd al-nadi*, p. 233.

[21] Ibn Qudama, *al-Mughni*, Vol. IV, p. 360; al-Ba'li, *al-Rawd al-nadi*, p. 233; al-Bahuti, *al-Rawd al-murbi'*, Vol. II, p. 190.

[22] Ibid.

[23] al-Bahuti, *al-Rawd al-murbi'*, Vol. II, p. 190.

[24] Ibn Qudama, *al-Mughni*, Vol. IV, p. 360.

Shafii and Layth ibn Sa'd do not share the Hanbali view on the repayment of a *qard* whose subject is a currency which became obsolete: for them, the lender receives back only the like of what he has lent, on the ground that the loaned currency has not suffered a defect but a decrease in value.

In principle, the place for repaying a *qard* is where the *qard* was concluded.[25] If the lender asks to be repaid in another country but the transportation of the object of the *qard* requires expenses, the borrower is not under the obligation to comply with the lender's request; but if the lender asks for the value in exchange, then his demand must be satisfied, for no extra expenses are involved in such a case. If it is the borrower who offers to pay the value in exchange in another place, the lender is entitled to refuse that offer, for he might suffer some loss when assuming transportation to the place where the *qard* was concluded.[26] If the object of the *qard* is money or any article the transportation of which does not entail expenses, payment may take place in another country if the lender so requests.[27] The borrower may also compel the lender to receive payment in a country other than the one where the *qard* was concluded, provided that no expenses are to be incurred for the transportation and provided that the country – and the roads – where payment is offered are safe.[28]

Malikis teach that the borrower enjoys two options in discharging a *qard*: either to give back the like (*al-mithl*) of that which he has borrowed or to give back the very property lent to him, whether or not a fungible article, provided it has kept its essential features. If this proviso is not fulfilled, and the borrowed article undergoes transformation, then the borrower is under obligation to repay the like.[29]

The lender is not obliged to accept payment of the *qard* at a place different from the normal place of payment (i.e. the place where the *qard* was concluded, unless otherwise agreed) unless the object of the *qard* is gold, silver or jewellery, provided it is light. But if its weight is burdensome, or if there is a fear (of the road) then the lender is not compelled to receive payment in a place different from the place where the *qard* was concluded.[30] Similarly the borrower cannot be compelled to discharge the *qard* at a place different from the place where the *qard* was concluded.[31]

Shafiis hold that both fungible and non-fungible commodities, provided they are in circulation, may be the object of a *qard*. As for fungible commodities,

25 Ibid. 26 Ibid.

27 Ibid., p. 361; al-Bahuti, *al-Rawd al-murbi'*, Vol. II, p. 191.

28 al-Ba'li, *al-Rawd al-nadi*, p. 234; al-Bahuti, *al-Rawd al-murbi'*, Vol. II, p. 191.

29 Ibn Juzay, *Qawanin*, p. 316; Jaziri, *al-Fiqh 'ala al-madhahib*, Vol. II, p. 343; al-Dardir, *al-Sharh*, Vol. III, p. 296.

30 al-Dardir, *al-Sharh*, p. 296; al-Kashnawi, *Ashal al-madarik sharh irshad al-salik fi fiqh imam al-a' imma Malik*, Vol. II, pp. 318–19.

31 al-Kashnawi, *Ashal al-madarik*, Vol. II, p. 318.

the like (*al-mithl*) should be given back, whether currency or otherwise. When the subject of the *qard* is a non-fungible article, there are two opinions on how to discharge the contract of loan: the first opinion says that it is acceptable to give back the value rather than the like, and the other one that the borrower should give back an article similar to the object of the *qard* in characteristics and appearance.[32] In the event of the borrowed article being currency, other than gold or silver, which becomes obsolete, the borrower is under an obligation to give back the like provided that its value has not become negligible, otherwise he should return the value nearest to that obtaining at the time of claiming back the debt.[33]

If the *qard* took place in Egypt and its subject was dirhams (silver coins) and the lender and borrower meet in Mecca and the lender asks to be repaid, the borrower is obliged to comply with that request. If it is the borrower who offers payment, the lender must also accept, for there is no loss in taking the dirhams.[34] But if the object of the *qard* is food remitted to the borrower in Egypt and then the lender and borrower meet in Mecca and the lender asks to have similar food back, the borrower is free not to comply with such a request, for food in Mecca is more expensive than in Egypt. If it is the borrower who asks the lender to take it back (in Mecca), the lender may decline, for he is entitled to refuse to bear the expenses of transportation to the place where the *qard* was concluded. Of course, the lender and the borrower may always decide to agree on such a matter,[35] or the lender may ask to receive the value of the object of *qard* as assessed in the country where the *qard* was concluded.[36]

Ibadis. For the Ibadis, the rule is that the object of the *qard* should be well defined and ascertainable, so that when the time comes to discharge the *qard* repayment shall represent exactly what was remitted to the borrower in the first instance with no uncertainty (*gharar*) or fear of *riba*.[37] In principle, the borrowed article *in specie* (*al-ʿayn*) may be given back, or the like (*al-mithl*) or the value in exchange (*al-ʿiwad*). But giving back an article of a genus different from the one to which the borrowed article belongs *is* accepted, provided that it is not a prerequisite of the *qard*.[38]

When the transportation of the object of the *qard* entails expenses, the borrower, according to one opinion, should discharge his debt at the place where the *qard* was concluded and according to another opinion in any place of his choice, for the *qard* is a personal obligation; but if the object of the

32 al-Shirazi, *al-Muhadhdhab*, Vol. I, p. 304.
33 Jaziri, *al-Fiqhʿala al-madhahib*, Vol. II, p. 342.
34 al-Shirazi, *al-Muhadhdhab*, Vol. I, pp. 304–5.
35 Ibid.
36 Ibid; *Fatawa al-Ramli* in the margin of the book of *al-Fatawa al-kubra al-fiqhiyya* by al-Haythami, Vol. II, p. 169.
37 al-Salimi, *Jawhar al-nizam*, 1344 A.H. edn, p. 385.
38 Ibid., pp. 384–5; al-Shammakhi, *al-Idah*, Vol. III, pp. 414ff.

qard is banned by the authorities then the borrower is entitled to discharge his debt wherever it is in his power to do so. Claims whose transportation does not entail expenses, may be discharged at any place. As for chattels (*'urud*), such as wheat, barley or any kind of grain, repayment should be made in the location where the transaction was concluded. Another opinion holds that repayment can be made in any country provided that prices are the same.[39]

Is the lender entitled to derive any advantage from the *qard*?

Hanafis. For the Hanafis a *qard* should not, in principle, provide the lender with any advantage. This applies only if the advantage is agreed concurrently with the contract of *qard* for it is then an increase with no lawful basis and is deemed to be *riba*.[40] If, on the other hand, the advantage is not pre-agreed, or even (for some Hanafi authors) not stipulated in the contract of *qard*, it is not reprehensible for the lender to receive at a later stage more or better than he has lent, as it is permissible, though not recommended, for him to accept a gift from the borrower.[41]

A term giving time for repayment is not binding in a contract of *qard* whether stipulated in the contract itself or agreed afterwards.[42]

Hanbalis reassert that *qard* is a charitable act and should remain so. If an increase, whether in the quality or in the quantity, is stipulated that would alter the *qard*'s objective, for example a *qard* which is accompanied by an increase in favour of the lender or by a condition to the lender's advantage, such as the lender securing for himself the right to stay in the borrower's premises or the right to buy a property which belongs to the borrower, it is unlawful. A gift stipulated in the contract of *qard* is also unlawful; similarly it is unlawful that, prior to the repayment of the *qard*, the borrower gives the lender a gift, unless such a gift is deemed part of the repayment or unless that kind of gift was customary between the lender and the borrower.[43] If, on the other hand, it is stipulated in the contract of *qard* that repayment shall be less than what was taken and if the object of *qard* is a property susceptible of *riba* (*mal ribawi*), that also is forbidden, for the reason that it destroys the equality of the countervalues. Thus, stipulating that less, or that more, shall be given back to discharge the *qard* are equally unlawful. According to Ibn Quadama, some of Shafi'i's companions do deem lawful the repayment of less.[44]

39 al-Shammakhi, *al-Idah*, Vol. III, pp. 410–11.
40 al-Kasani, *Bada'i'*, Vol. VII, p. 395; Jaziri, *al-Fiqh 'ala al-madhahib*, Vol. II, p. 340.
41 Ibid.
42 al-Kasani, *Bada'i'*, Vol. VII, p. 396.
43 Ibn Qudama, *al-Mughni*, Vol. IV, pp. 354–6.
44 Ibid., p. 357.

Nevertheless, if an advantage is willingly granted to the lender *after* settlement and not before, or not as a condition, that is lawful. If in this connection a better thing is given back in repayment of the *qard*, that is also lawful, for the Prophet did so.[45]

For the Hanbalis, repayment of a *qard* is immediately due at the lender's request, even when the latter has granted the borrower a respite, for *qard* is a contract whereby not only is inequality of the countervalues forbidden, but also any term giving time for repayment.[46] The lender is even entitled to request repayment forthwith and in bulk even when the *qard* was handed over in instalments.[47] As reported by Ibn Qudama,[48] compulsory repayment of the *qard* on demand is a concept advocated by Abu Hanifa, Shafiʿi, al-Awzaʿi and others but not by Maliki, as we will see below.

Malikis. For the adherents of the Maliki school, it is unlawful that a *qard* agreement should stipulate conditions to the lender's advantage, such as lending imperfect wheat with the proviso that good quality shall be given back.[49] It is also forbidden that the lender should accept a gift from the borrower, except if it was customary for the lender, prior to the *qard*, to receive such a gift, or if after the *qard* an event occurs giving a good reason for the gift, such as marriage; otherwise no gift caused by the *qard*, whether apparent or hidden, is allowed.[50] This prohibition is not restricted to a gift as such but applies to any advantage or benefit that the lender might secure out of the *qard*, such as riding the borrower's mule, eating at his table, drinking his coffee or even taking advantage of the shade of his walls when any such activity is performed not as a sign of esteem but because of the *qard*.[51] If the advantage or benefit is for the borrower, such as granting him a rebate when the *qard* is discharged, that is lawful; if it is to both the lender's and the borrower's advantage or benefit, that is acceptable only in case of necessity (*darura*);[52] this applies also to the bill of exchange (*suftaja*).[53]

[45] al-Bahuti, *al-Rawd al-murbiʿ*, Vol. II, p. 190; al-Baʿli, *al-Rawd al-nadi*, p. 234.

[46] al-Bahuti, *al-Rawd al-murbiʿ*, Vol. II, p. 190; al-Baʿli, *al-Rawd al-nadi*, pp. 233–4; Ibn Qudama, *al-Mughni*, Vol. IV, p. 349.

[47] Ibn Qudama, *al-Mughni*, Vol. IV, p. 349.

[48] Ibid.

[49] Jaziri, *al-Fiqh ʿala al-madhahib*, Vol. II, p. 343; al-Kashnawi, *Ashal al-madarik*, Vol. II, p. 318.

[50] Jaziri, *al-Fiqh ʿala al-madhahib*, Vol. II, p. 343; Ibn Juzay, *Qawanin*, p. 316.

[51] al-Dardir, *al-Sharh*, Vol. III, p. 293.

[52] Ibid., p. 295; al-Kashnawi, *Ashal al-madarik*, Vol. II, p. 318.

[53] *Suftaja* is described as being the loan of money to "A", with the agreement that "A" will repay it to "B" in another country, in order to avoid the risk of transport. Hanafis accept the concept of *suftaja* with aversion (*karahiyya*), (al-Kasani, *Bada'iʿ*, Vol. VII, pp. 395–6). Hanbalis deem *suftaja* as being lawful, provided it is agreed following the conclusion of the *qard* and not as a prerequisite of the *qard* (Ibn Qudama, *al-Mughni*, Vol. IV, p. 356) as do the Shafiis (al-Shirazi, *al-Muhadhdhab*, Vol. I, p. 304) and, apparently, the Ibadis (al-Salimi, *Jawhar al-nizam*, pp. 384–5).

Contrary to the other schools, the Malikis teach that a term for delayed repayment stipulated in a *qard* agreement is binding, which means that the lender cannot ask for payment if the term has not yet reached maturity. They see no reason why the following Quranic verse should not apply to such a loan: "Oh ye who believe, fulfil your Contracts" (s. V:1).[54] When the *qard* has a fixed repayment date, the borrower is obliged to repay it at maturity date even though he has not derived any benefit therefrom. When the *qard* has no fixed repayment date, there are two distinct possibilities: either there is a custom governing the loaned article and directing that it should be given back at a certain time, such as the loan of wheat which is normally repaid at the following crop, or there is no custom in respect of the loaned article; in such a case the borrower is allowed to keep it until such time as he makes use of it as generally accepted for articles of the kind.[55] Finally it is deemed unlawful to agree that part of the debt shall be discounted if the borrower discharges the remaining part before maturity date is reached.[56]

Shafiis. A *qard* which gives an advantage to the lender is unlawful, such as giving back more in quantity or a better quality.[57] If the lender agrees to be repaid less than he has given, some Shafii scholars disallow such a rebate and some others assent to it on the ground that accepting less does not alter the *qard*'s purpose, which is to assist the borrower.[58] If the borrower willingly and not as a prerequisite of the *qard*, or out of custom, gives back more or better than he has borrowed, or writes a bill of exchange (*suftaja*) or sells his house to the lender, that is allowed, for the Prophet himself discharged a loan of an animal by giving back a better one.[59]

At any moment, the lender has the right to ask for repayment and the borrower the right to discharge the *qard*, even though a delay was originally stipulated.[60]

Ibadis. It is unlawful for the lender, according to the Ibadi doctrine, to accept any increase on his claim, for it might have its cause in the *qard* itself. It is even said that eating at the debtor's table is *riba*, although such an opinion is qualified as follows: if it is customary that the lender and borrower eat at each other's table, then eating is permitted; equally it is permitted for the lender, if he feels that he will not have the opportunity to reciprocate the borrower's invitation, to remit something from his claim, provided such claim has nothing to do with a *bay' salam*.[61]

[54] 'Ali Khafif, *Ahkam al-mu'amalat al-Shar'iyya*, p. 287.
[55] al-Dardir, *al-Sharh*, Vol. III, pp. 295–6; Jaziri, *al-Fiqh 'ala al-madhahib*, Vol. II, p. 343.
[56] al-Kashnawi, *Ashal al-madarik*, Vol. II, p. 319.
[57] al-Shirazi, *al-Muhadhdhab*, Vol. I, p. 304; Jaziri, *al-Fiqh 'ala al-madhahib*, Vol. II, p. 342.
[58] Ibid. [59] Ibid.
[60] al-Nawawi, *Minhaj al-talibin*, p. 196 (trans. E. C. Howard).
[61] al-Shammakhi, *al-Idah*, Vol. III, pp. 416–17.

As a general rule, if the borrower wants to give back more or better than he has borrowed, willingly and not as a prerequisite of the *qard*, he is entitled to do so.[62] When the object of a *qard* is an animal, it is always lawful to give back better, as did the Prophet.[63] In principle, the lender is not entitled to accept less than the amount of the *qard*, but this strict view is not shared by all Ibadi scholars, who base their opinion on the reasoning that the borrower and the lender are both free to accept either an increase or a reduction, as a gift between themselves.[64]

Ibadi scholars lean strongly towards considering a term for delayed repayment in a loan agreement as not binding.[65]

3 *Qard* with a *riba* stipulation: valid or not?

The question now arises of what is the effect of a special clause or condition involving *riba* on the validity of the whole *qard* agreement. We can best answer this by considering it as part of a broader problem, which was stated by N. Coulson[66] in the following terms: "[In Islamic Law] each nominate contract is strictly, and usually simply, defined in terms of its purpose and effect, and the question is how far, if at all, may the parties vary this rigid scheme by introducing agreed special terms as appendages to the particular nominate contract they are purporting to conclude."

Once the validity or the nullity of a special term or condition (*shart*, pl. *shurut*) is ascertained, the next question is whether a special condition that is deemed void by Sharia standards can be severed from the agreement as if non-existent, leaving the transaction itself valid, or does it, on the contrary, completely nullify the whole transaction? As is generally the case, the schools of law that are the object of our scrutiny did not come up with one answer, as the following survey of their teachings indicates.[67]

Hanafis. Pursuant to a general principle laid down by the Hanafi *fiqh*, a special condition is allowed if it is necessary to the contract itself (*min muqtadayat al-ʿaqd*): for example the vendor retaining possession of the object of the sale until the time he receives payment; or if it is appropriate to the contract (*mulaʾim liʾl-ʿaqd*), such as the vendor asking for a pledge to secure payment of a sale price; or if the condition is customary to the inhabitants of the place where the contract is concluded.

62 al-Salimi, *Jawhar al-nizam*, 1344 A.H. edn, p. 384.

63 al-Shammakhi, *al-Idah*, Vol. III, pp. 417–18.

64 Ibid., p. 417.

65 Ibid., p. 411 note; al-Salimi, *Jawhar al-nizam*, p. 385.

66 N. Coulson, *Commercial Law in the Gulf States*, p. 51.

67 For other details on the problem of special conditions (*shurut*) see: N. Coulson, *Commercial Law*, pp. 50–5; N. Saleh, *The General Principles of Saudi Arabian and Omani Company Laws*, pp. 68–78 and Y. Linant de Bellefonds, *Traîté de droit Musulman comparé*, Vol. I, pp. 224–42, Paris 1965.

Transactions which entail an exchange of countervalues in terms of finance or otherwise, as in the case of a sale, partition of real property, lease, *waqf* and so on, are cancelled by effect of a void special condition. There is one exception: if the void special condition is of no advantage to any of the contracting parties, such as the sale of an animal with the condition that its new owner shall not resell it, then the condition is cancelled but not the contract. In contrast, a transaction which does *not* involve an exchange of countervalues in terms of finance or otherwise, as in the case of a loan, gift, pledge or will, is unaffected by a void special condition: the latter is cancelled but the transaction remains.[68]

Hanbalis. About the Hanbalis it was said, not without reason, that the validating of special conditions is the rule and that makes it easier to determine when a special condition is deemed void under their *fiqh*. That is normally the case when the special condition falls under either of the two following categories:

(a) If it conflicts with the objective or the essence of the transaction, such as when the vendor requires from the buyer that he shall not sell or otherwise dispose of what he has acquired. The effect of such a void special condition on the contract itself is limited, according to a large number of Hanbali scholars; the condition is cancelled but the contract remains.[69] Pursuant to that teaching, a loan agreement is not invalidated by a void special condition it contains: the condition is simply deleted therefrom.[70]

(b) If the special condition is contrary to a specific prohibition in the Sharia, such as when the Prophet disallowed the presence of two conditions in one contract. The two conditions which are proscribed, according to the Hanbali interpretation, are those which bring an advantage for one of the contracting parties without being necessitated by or appropriate to the contract itself. When such is the case the conditions as well as the contract are cancelled. The classic example of the combination of two such conditions in one contract is when the buyer of grain requires that the vendor mills it and carries it to him. But if the conditions, whether two or more, are necessary or appropriate to the contract itself, such as a sale made contingent upon the presentation of a pledge together with another security, then the conditions are valid.

Malikis. For the Malikis a special condition is void when it conflicts with the legal objective of a transaction, such as when a clause in a sale contract perpetuates the inalienability of the object of the sale. Also void is a condition which affects the sale price and aims at defeating the *riba* prohibition.[71] Whether the contract as a whole is cancelled, or only the void special condition, is contingent upon whether either *riba* or *gharar*, the two elements which make void a special condition, is material enough. When

[68] S. Mahmasani, *The General Theory*, pp. 461–2; S. Baz, *Sharh al-Majalla*, under Art. 83.
[69] al-Bahuti, *Kashshaf al-qina'*, Vol. III, pp. 193–4.
[70] Art. 745 of al-Qari's *Majallat al-ahkam al-shar'iyya*, ed. by Abu Sulayman and M.I. 'Ali.
[71] Y. Linant De Bellefonds, *Traité de droit Musulman comparé*, Vol. I, p. 239.

either *is* material, then the contract is cancelled as a whole; otherwise the void condition is severed from the contract.[72]

Ibadis. Their doctrine on special conditions can be summed up as follows:

(a) A special condition should not conflict with the objective of the contract (*ma yurad bi'l-ʿaqd*), otherwise the condition is void and cancels the whole contract according to one opinion – which, however, seems not to have remained unchallenged.[73]

(b) When a special condition directly relates to the object of the sale (*shart fi nafs al-mabiʿ*) – the sale contract being again used as the standard contract in Sharia – and when this special condition is well defined, to the advantage of the vendor, and furthermore the latter is entitled to benefit therefrom, taking into consideration the nature and objective of the transaction, then the condition and the contract are valid, such as when the vendor of a mule secures for himself the right to ride that mule up to a given town. In the event of this special condition *not* being well defined, owing to uncertainty (*gharar*) or want of knowledge (*jahl*) then the condition and the sale are void.[74] In the event of the vendor not being entitled to benefit from the special condition, then the condition is cancelled, whereas the contract remains valid.[75]

(c) When a special condition does not directly relate to the object of the sale, such as when the sale is completed against the remittance of a measure of barley, with the proviso that the buyer should mill the barley or should transport it to a certain place, that condition is void on acount of the want of knowledge (*jahl*) in respect of the price (it is not known how much of the sale price is constituted by the barley itself and how much by the milling and transport); if it is the buyer who requests of the vendor that *he* should mill or transport the barley, that also causes the collapse of the whole contract owing to the want of knowledge in respect of the subject-matter.[76]

As for the effect on the whole contract of a stipulation involving *riba*, the Ibadi authors seem to be of the opinion that the contracting parties should be restored to the respective situations they had before the contract, pursuant to the Quranic injunction, "If you repent you shall have your capital sums", which is interpreted to mean that the *ribawi* contract is repealed.[77]

Shafiis. Shafii teaching with regard to special conditions (*shurut*) is particularly complex owing to all the distinctions it contains and also because of some conflicting *responsa* found in the traditional Shafii manuals. Despite these difficulties we have attempted the following summary:

(a) A sale accompanied by a special condition actually forming a separate agreement, such as the sale of a crop with the requirement that the vendor shall gather the harvest, is null because of the *gharar* (uncertainty) in respect of the

[72] Ibn Rushd, *Bidayat al-mujtahid*, Vol. II, p. 160.
[73] al-Salimi, *Jawhar al-nizam*, 1344 A.H. edn, p. 346.
[74] al-Shammakhi, *al-Idah*, Vol. III, p. 78.
[75] Ibid., pp. 78–9. [76] Ibid., pp. 79–80.
[77] al-Shammakhi, *al-Idah*, Vol. III, pp. 21–2; al-Salimi, *Jawhar al-nizam*, p. 324.

sale price and what proportion of it gathering the harvest constitutes. An additional ground for the nullity lies in the fact that the harvesting is required by the party (the prospective buyer) which is not yet the owner of the crop.[78]

(b) No special condition can change the essence of a nominate contract. Consequently a special condition which negates the buyer's right to take possession of the object of the sale or to give it back for defect, is deemed non-existent.[79] The effect of such nullity on the contract itself is not constant in the Shafii legal system. One view differentiates between transactions which strictly entail the mutual exchange of countervalues such as the sale contract, and all other transactions. In the first category, a special condition which attempts to change the essence of the contract is void, and produces the nullity of the contract. In the second category, such a special condition is void but the transaction often stands.[80]

(c) A special condition is valid if it is not intended to alter the essence of the contract and is connected with the legitimate interests of the parties, such as the vendor requiring a pledge or the buyer a specific attribute to be found in the object of the sale.[81]

(d) A special condition is null if, although it is not intended to alter the essence of the contract, it is *not* connected with the legitimate interests of the parties. When the nullity of such a condition does not lead to dispute in direct connection with the contract intended by the contracting parties, e.g. the condition that from the time of the sale the buyer would eat only a specific food, the contract remains unaffected. But when the nullity of such specific condition does lead to a dispute in direct connection with the contract, such as is the case when the buyer requires the vendor's guarantee of compensation should he resell what he has acquired at a loss, then the contract as a whole is annulled.[82]

As for a loan agreement which contains a clause importing *riba*, here again Shafii authors do not come out with a clear-cut answer. For some, a loan agreement impaired with *riba* is void: for, first, the Prophet himself has said that "Any *qard* which stipulates an advantage to the lender is *riba*"; and secondly, when a *qard* is made contingent upon a condition which is not fulfilled, it is considered only just to cancel the whole agreement. The opposite view is also sustained, on the ground that the objective of *qard* is charity and this objective can only be enhanced by removing the void special conditions and retaining the agreement.[83]

4 *Riba*'s narrowed scope

For many, *riba* is no more and no less than the prohibited payment or receipt of interest on loans of money. This is an incorrect view and, in theory at least, *riba* has a much wider field of application. *Riba* may pervert any

78 al-Rafi'i, *Fath al-'aziz* in margin of al-Nawawi's *Sharh al-Muhadhdhab*, Vol. VIII, p. 195.
79 Ibid., pp. 204–5.
80 al-Haythami, *al-Fatawa*, Vol. II, p. 229.
81 al-Rafi'i, *Fath al-'aziz*, in al-Nawawi, *Sharh al-Muhadhdhab*, pp. 204–5.
82 Ibid.
83 al-Shirazi, *al-Muhadhdhab*, Vol. I, p. 304.

transaction which involves the exchange of two or more countervalues if and when certain conditions are met; these conditions vary from one school of law to another; they also change depending on whether the exchange is to take place immediately or with deferment. All that we have already seen in detail. Barter and money exchange are among the transactions that are vulnerable to *riba*; and sale is, too, when currency is not one of the countervalues. But today that sort of sale is hardly practised; barter is uncommon and money exchange operations can take place without deferment, thus averting the risk of *riba al-nasi'a*. The deferred payment of a sale price is deemed valid by most scholars, even when it is accompanied by an increase in that price. Moreover, a carefully contrived range of legal stratagems (*hiyal*) under which usurious transactions can take place developed in countries where the Hanafi and Shafii schools are prevalent. Indeed these legal stratagems are not acceptable to other schools of law, but that had no practical significance until recently, for the countries where *hiyal* were rejected did not have enough economic leverage to deprive the legal stratagems of an important field of application. That is no longer the case, with the discovery of great quantities of oil in the very countries where *hiyal* are banned.

This is to say that, practically speaking, popular belief is not far from reality and the censure of *riba* in practice amounts simply to the forbidding of payment and receipt of interest on loans of money. We recall that the Quranic verses in relation to *riba* spoke of loan agreements. Barter was accounted among the transactions susceptible to *riba* by the Prophet's Tradition, as were, by Islamic jurisprudence (*fiqh*), all sorts of transactions which cause two or more countervalues to change hands. This is not to suggest that the structure of *fiqh* in relation to *riba* is obsolete, but merely that it has lost some of its interest through a change of circumstances which has confined *riba*'s field of application to the loan of money first mentioned in the Quran – the fundamental source of the prohibition, which retains all its importance.

CHAPTER 3

Gharar (uncertainty, risk, speculation)

I Introduction

Gharar, unlike *riba*, has in process of time had its field of application greatly widened. Concern for protecting human beings from their own folly and extravagance is an important feature of the Quran, and it consequently proscribed games of hazard (s. II:219 and s. V:93), thus providing religious grounds for suspicion of *gharar*. Tradition added to this the result of the Prophet's vast experience as a merchant and his deep knowledge of human nature, for it did not escape him that it is not uncommon, in secular transactions, for one of the parties to be stronger than the other, or perhaps cleverer or more experienced; so the disadvantaged party is in need of some kind of protection and guidance before an agreement is concluded or a bargain struck. This was even more the case during the Prophet's time, when a substantial difference in terms of enlightenment and development existed between bedouins and townsmen, and even between townsmen belonging to different settlements. One established hadith tells that Muhammad forbade a transaction known as *talaqi al-rukban*, which is a sale whereby a townsman meets a tribesman outside the market place and buys the tribesman's goods at a price cheaper than the price prevailing in the market, thus taking advantage of the seller's ignorance of the market price.

This idea of protecting the weak against exploitation by the strong led to the elaboration of a rule of general application, commanding that any transaction should be devoid of uncertainty and speculation, and this, according to learned men and legal scholars, could only be secured by the contracting parties' having perfect knowledge of the countervalues intended to be exchanged as a result of their transaction, otherwise there is an unacceptable degree of *gharar*. Thus, what was intended to be a religious precept was transformed into a worldly rule which affects a great proportion of secular transactions. Far from having its scope narrowed by a change of circumstances, the question of *gharar* pervades a number of contemporary operations which were not contemplated or at any rate not common during the Prophet's time. This is to say that transactions and contracts relating to insurance and assurance, to life annuity, to the stock exchange market and generally speaking all sorts of transactions where the subject-matter, the price or both, are not determined and fixed in advance, are under a suspicion of *gharar* according to Sharia standards.

But, as is often the case, the fusion of theory and practice was here, again, never completely achieved, if we except a comparatively short period of time before and following Muhammad's death. Consequently, risk and uncertainty were not fully eliminated from secular transactions: these, from the nineteenth century onwards, were to follow a more or less foreign pattern and to be governed by Western-inspired rules. Moreover, just about the only tribute paid to Islamic law was an emphatic statement to the effect that Islamic law was not betrayed in those transactions – even though the reality was to contradict this assertion.

Nevertheless, Islamic law was kept very much alive in the Muslims' conscience if not in their business. Today they see an opportunity to live in conformity with their beliefs, and all signs indicate that many will grasp the occasion. The inevitable result is that a number of contemporary transactions tainted with *gharar* will be submitted anew to a Sharia test which cannot be passed by a mere declaration of good intent.

2 Definition of *gharar*

Most cases of *gharar* brought to the attention of early Muslim jurists are drawn from sale contracts, whether real or hypothetical. This is because the sale contract is regarded by *fiqh* as the typical contract, the one on which other contracts are modelled. Nevertheless rules and principles derived from sale examples are also relevant, *mutatis mutandis*, to secular transactions in general.

Few traditional authors have felt the need to define *gharar* or to outline its ambit in precise words. The few definitions we have are generally incomplete and do not convey the comprehensive meaning expected from definitions. Even an outstanding jurist such as Ibn Qayyim al-Jawziyya[1] described *gharar*, rather briefly, as being the subject-matter that the vendor is not in a position to hand over to the buyer, whether this subject-matter is in existence or not. However, it is only fair to say that Ibn Qayyim was concerned only to challenge those who had mistaken *gharar* for non-existence (*ʿadam*) and who erroneously saw the reason for the prohibition of *gharar* as the non-existence of the subject-matter, rather than the risk of uncertainty which casts a shadow on the subject-matter.

Another author[2] equated *gharar* with an uncontrolled subject-matter, such as a bird in the air or fish in the water. But here again the definition was an answer to those who had confused *gharar* with the unknown (*majhul*).

[1] Ibn Qayyim al-Jawziyya, *Iʿlam al-muwaqqiʿin*, Vol. I, pp. 357–61.

[2] al-Qarafi, *al-Furuq*, Vol. III, pp. 265–6, Cairo 1344–46 A.H.

Majhul is itself described by the same author as being an existing subject-matter whose characteristics are unknown, such as selling what is hidden in one's sleeve.

Sanhuri[3] adopted more or less *al-Furuq*'s definition of *gharar*, but added to it the essential element of want of knowledge (*jahl*), saying that *jahl* brings about *gharar* in the following circumstances: when it is not known whether the subject-matter exists or, if it exists, whether it can be handed over to the buyer, or when want of knowledge affects the identification of the genus or species to which the subject-matter belongs or its characteristics, its quantum, its identity, or its condition remaining satisfactory. Want of knowledge with regard to the date of future performance, if any, also generates *gharar*.

Ibn Juzay,[4] a Maliki author, obviously aware of the difficulty of defining *gharar*, gave a list of ten cases which constitute, in his view, a forbidden *gharar*. These cases are described as follows.

(a) Difficulty in putting the buyer in possession of the subject-matter; such as the sale of a stray animal or the young still unborn when the mother is not part of the sale.
(b) Want of knowledge (*jahl*) with regard to the price or the subject-matter, such as the vendor saying to the potential buyer: "I sell you what is in my sleeve."
(c) Want of knowledge with regard to the characteristics of the price or of the subject-matter, such as the vendor saying to the potential buyer: "I sell you a piece of cloth which is in my home"; or the sale of an article without the buyer inspecting or the seller describing it.[5]
(d) Want of knowledge with regard to the quantum of the price or the quantity of the subject-matter, such as an offer to sell "at today's price" or "at the market price".
(e) Want of knowledge with regard to the date of future performance, such as an offer to sell when a stated person enters the room or when a stated person dies.
(f) Two sales in one transaction, such as selling one article at two different prices, one for cash and one for credit, or selling two different articles at one price, one for immediate remittance and one for a deferred one.
(g) The sale of what is not expected to revive, such as the sale of a sick animal.
(h) *Bay' al-hasah*, which is a type of sale whose outcome is determined by the throwing of a stone.
(i) *Bay' munabadha*, which is a sale performed by the vendor throwing a cloth at the buyer and achieving the sale transaction without giving the buyer the opportunity for properly examining the object of the sale.
(j) *Bay' mulamasa*, where the bargain is struck by touching the object of the sale without examining it.

It is Ibn Rushd, another Maliki author of the sixth century after the Hijra, who tried to define *gharar* in a comprehensive but nevertheless short formula. However, it is still necessary to combine two excerpts from his well-

[3] Sanhuri, *Masadir al-haqq*, Vol. III, p. 49.
[4] Ibn Juzay, *Qawanin*, pp. 282–3.
[5] Sale according to description is reviewed below (pp. 67ff.).

known treatise, *Bidayat al-mujtahid*,[6] in order to achieve the following definition: *gharar* in sale transactions causes the buyer to suffer damage (*ghubn*) and is the result of a want of knowledge (*jahl*) which affects either the price or the subject-matter. *Gharar* is averted if both the price and the subject-matter are known to be in existence, if their characteristics are known, if their amount is determined, if the parties have such control over them as to make sure that the exchange shall take place and, finally, if the date of future performance, if any, is defined. Shaikh ʿAmir ibn ʿAli al-Shammakhi,[7] the Ibadi author of the seventh century after the Hijra, adopted not too different a definition of *gharar*. For both these authors and for other early scholars, a material want of knowledge in either the subject-matter or in the price can produce *gharar*.

Coming to modern times, the majority of contemporary Muslim authors have studied *gharar* from the single angle of the subject-matter and virtually neglected the effects of *gharar* on the price – not surprisingly, perhaps, in view of the intimate relation of this problem with the concept of *riba*. I do not intend to follow this trend: I shall be examining *gharar* and its effects on both the subject-matter and the price, even though rather briefly for the latter case, for the study of *riba* must by now have answered many of the questions that *gharar* raises when it affects the price.

On the basis of the above definitions, observance of the following three rules should, in principle, avert *gharar* in any given transaction:

(a) There should be no want of knowledge (*jahl*) regarding the existence of the exchanged countervalues.
(b) There should be no want of knowledge (*jahl*) regarding the characteristics of the exchanged countervalues or the identification of their species or knowledge of their quantities or of the date of future performance, if any.
(c) Control of the parties over the exchanged countervalues should be effective.

Although these requisites are certainly urged by Islamic *fiqh*, they are not without important qualifications and exceptions, which will be examined in detail in the following three sections. (For the sources of the prohibition of *gharar* in Sharia, see Appendix 2.)

3 Avoiding want of knowledge (*jahl*) concerning the existence of the exchanged countervalues

The subject-matter in bilateral transactions

An overwhelming majority of traditional Muslim scholars have nullified bilateral transactions whose subject-matters are non-existent (*maʿdum*)

6 Ibn Rushd, *Bidayat al-mujtahid*, Vol. II, pp. 148 and 172.
7 al-Shammakhi, *al-Idah*, Vol. III, p. 54.

when they are concluded. It was obvious to them that what is non-existent involves necessarily a strong element of *gharar*, for it is uncertain whether the non-existent object would ever materialize, or in what condition and state it would materialize.[8] Despite this straightforward condemnation some of these scholars qualified the result they had apparently reached, in one way or another. Thus, the Maliki author Ibn Rushd said that in case of necessity (*darura*) and when the future inception of the subject-matter is certain, such as when during one harvest fruits are produced in continuing and connected succession, a sale contract of the whole harvest would be valid.[9] Shafii authors tolerate *gharar* in case of need (*haja*) and when *gharar* cannot be averted except with great difficulty.[10] Ibadis tolerate *gharar* if it is immaterial, or in case of necessity.[11]

The above exceptions did not carry enough weight to change perceptibly the views of the different schools of law. For them non-existence (*ʿadam*) amounted to *gharar*. It was no longer *gharar* which was the foundation of the prohibition but non-existence. However, it was also advocated that if the subject-matter was non-existent in its essence (*asl*) at the time the contract was concluded, the contract was void, even though its future existence was in no doubt; but if the essence (*asl*) was in existence at the date of agreement, some nominate contracts were deemed valid under certain circumstances. Examples of such contracts were the sale of fruits and agricultural products, the contract of manufacture, and *bayʿ salam*.

These qualifications and exceptions, and also a remarkable talent for legal problems, prompted Ibn Qayyim al-Jawziyya to denounce the confusion between uncertainty and non-existence. He wrote in one of his treatises:[12] "There is no mention either in the Book of Allah or in the Sunna or in the Companions' Tradition of anything to the effect that the sale of what is non-existent is prohibited. . . What is in the Sunna is the prohibition of selling certain articles which are non-existent as there is a prohibition of selling other articles which actually exist. The motive behind the prohibition is not the existence or non-existence but, as in the Sunna, the sale producing uncertainty and that is what the vendor is not in a position to deliver, whether or not it exists. . . The vendor's obligation is to deliver the subject-matter of the sale; if he is not in a position to do so, this amounts to *gharar*,

[8] The arbitration clause is a good present-day illustration of this principle; despite assertion to the contrary by some modernist law authors, arbitration clauses cannot be reconciled with Sharia tenets for a twofold reason, namely (1) an arbitration clause amounts to an undertaking to execute in the future and that is essentially revocable; and (2) an undertaking to resort to arbitration if and when needed is given before the existence of any dispute, and that is in principle unacceptable by Sharia standards (Samir Saleh, *Commercial Arbitration in the Arab Middle East*, pp. 48ff.).

[9] Ibn Rushd, *Bidayat al-mujtahid*, Vol. II, p. 156.

[10] al-Nawawi, *al-Majmuʿ, sharh al-Muhadhdhab*, Vol. IX, p. 258.

[11] al-Shammakhi, *al-Idah*, Vol. III, pp. 68–9.

[12] Ibn Qayyim al-Jawziyya, *Iʿlam al-muwaqqiʿin*, Vol. I, pp. 357–61.

risk and gambling. . . The prohibited non-existence is not prompted by non-existence itself but by *gharar*."

Dr ʿAbd al-Razzaq Sanhuri,[13] the contemporary Egyptian jurist, was prompt to grasp the occasion provided by such great authority as Ibn Qayyim; he tried to break the deadlock that traditional scholars have produced, caused primarily by their use of hypothetical examples, and differentiated between "what is non-existent" and "what is non-existent at the time being but shall necessarily occur in the future". Dr Sanhuri deplored the fact that traditional scholars had no regard to the future existence of the non-existent article before they issued their condemnation. He advocated that a distinction should be made between, on the one hand, the case where the non-existent article will certainly come into existence, thus excluding the danger of *gharar*, and on the other hand, the case where the future existence of the article in question is a mere possibility, thus involving the notion of *gharar*: here the fate of the transaction will be determined according to the degree of *gharar* involved. Sanhuri ended his own interpretation of *gharar* by saying that Islamic law does not forbid the sale of what is non-existent except when such a sale involves a material element of *gharar*. The foundation of the prohibition is exorbitant (*fahish*) *gharar*, which invalidates a given transaction whether or not the subject-matter is in existence. If *gharar* is slight or immaterial (*yasir*), the transaction is valid whether or not the subject-matter is in existence. The rationale behind the prohibition is not dealing with non-existence *per se* but the fact that this dealing introduces a significant element of *gharar*. It remains to be seen whether Sanhuri's interpretation of *gharar* will be followed by other contemporary Muslim authors. What can assist in reaching a consensus over this subject is a proper examination of the exceptions to the principle of prohibition unanimously adopted by forerunners of different schools of law.

Before undertaking such an examination let us follow another contemporary Lebanese jurist, Dr Subhi Mahmasani, in the distinction he made between the subject-matter being an object *in rem* and the subject-matter being work (*ʿamal*) or use (*manfaʿa*).[14] In the first instance, the rule that the subject-matter of a bilateral contract should be in existence at the time the contract is concluded finds its full scope of application. It is not so when work or use is the subject-matter, for these are necessarily non-existent at the time the contract is concluded but come progressively into being by the gradual implementation of the contract. A typical example of a contract involving use as a subject-matter is the hire contract, where the subject-matter materializes gradually by the lessee making use of the hired object. The

[13] Sanhuri, *Masadir al-haqq*, Vol. III, pp. 31–41.

[14] S. Mahmasani, *The General Theory of the Law of Obligations and Contracts under Islamic Jurisprudence*, Vol. I, pp. 326ff.

same applies to other kinds of transactions whose object is use (*manfaʿa*) such as a guarantee of debts or a power of attorney.[15]

These types of transaction were tolerated by Islamic law on the ground of equity (*istihsan*) and necessity (*darura*), and in some cases because they were mentioned in the Quran or practised by the Prophet himself. Nevertheless, Islamic jurisprudence endeavoured to curtail the risk of *gharar* by setting up rules regarding the use (*manfaʿa*) and the fee for the use. If the hire contract is taken as an example indicative of other transactions of the same kind, it becomes clear that use (*manfaʿa*) should be determined in a way which prevents a dispute arising. Knowledge of the use and knowledge of the hire payments are two requisites for the validity of a hire contract.[16] This is modelled on the sale contract, which is not valid unless the subject is determined in quantity and quality; in this manner a hire contract is not valid unless its use is determined. Only an immaterial want of knowledge (*jahl*), i.e. a want of knowledge which is not sufficient to generate a dispute, is tolerated, otherwise the contract is invalid.

Knowledge of the use is secured either by indication of its subject-matter, such as engaging a carpenter for the making of specified doors, or by indicating the duration of the contract, such as employing a workman for a whole year.[17] When both duration and task are determined in order to put a pressure of time on the hired person, there is a controversy among scholars about the validity of the hire contract; some scholars[18] refuse to recognize the legality of a hire contract where both duration and task are determined, for the reason that this might increase the element of *gharar* already in existence in a hire contract, whereas others[19] have no objection to the determination of both task and duration. When in a hire contract either the use or the fee is unknown, this contract is void.[20] In a hire contract which is deemed void, the employed person is entitled to a fair payment (*ujrat al-mithl*) whether small or substantial. Only Abu Hanifa and his two companions taught that this fair remuneration should not exceed the fee mentioned in the void contract. This view is not shared by all other schools of law, which consider that the assessment of the fair payment is not limited by what is indicated in the void contract.[21]

15 Ibid.

16 Dr Sharaf ibn ʿAli al-Sharif, *al-Ijara al-warida ʿala ʿamal al-insan*, p. 102.

17 Ibid., p. 103.

18 The majority of Hanafis (al-Sarakhsi, *al-Mabsut*, Vol. XVI, p. 44); Shafiis (al-Shirazi, *al-Muhadhdhab*, Vol. I, pp. 402–3); Hanbalis (al-Bahuti, *Sharh Muntaha al-iradat* Vol. II, pp. 355, 365 and 366); Malikis (Ibn Juzay, *Qawanin*, p. 302).

19 Abu Yusuf among the Hanafis (*al-Fatawa al-ʿAlamgiriyya*, Vol. IV, p. 423). One report on Ibn Hanbal. A few Shafiis and Malikis are not opposed to the determination of both task and duration. Ibadis seem also not to oppose the determination of both task and duration (al-Basyani, *Mukhtasar*, p. 287).

20 al-Sharif, *al-Ijara*, p. 325.

21 Ibid., pp. 328–30.

The effects of *gharar* on gratuitous contracts and unilateral transactions

It would be wrong to assume that *gharar* corrupts nothing but bilateral contracts for exchange of countervalues; in fact, *gharar* can also impair gratuitous contracts and unilateral transactions, though to a lesser degree.[22] This is substantiated by examining the impact of *gharar* on three chosen examples, namely donation, wills and power of attorney.

Donation

For the Malikis, *gharar* has no effect on donations; it is valid to donate objects whose sale would be invalid, such as an escaped animal, or fruit before it shows signs of readiness.[23] The Ibadi view is fairly close to the Maliki one: an unborn animal can be the subject-matter of a donation, and donation of what is subject to want of knowledge (*majhul*) is valid, according to a number of Ibadi authors, provided that the want of knowledge can be dispelled by describing the subject-matter.[24] This is not what the Shafiis and the other Sunni schools teach: for them, *gharar* impairs all contracts, whether a price is involved or not, with minor exceptions as regards gratuitous transactions, such as for the Shafiis the lawfulness of donating fruit before it shows signs of readiness.[25]

Hanafis require that the subject-matter of a donation be known and determined (Article 858, *Majalla*). They do not allow the donation of milk still in the udders or of uncut wool, but once milk and wool are set apart and remitted to the donee, that is valid, which would not be the case for a sale contract. Donating the unborn young of an animal is invalid, for it is not known whether it will be brought forth alive or dead.[26]

Under Hanbali teaching, although the donation of what is unknown (*majhul*), such as an unborn animal or milk in the udders is invalid, in some circumstances such as when the properties of two persons are intermingled in a way which makes their separate identification impossible, one of these persons may donate his property to the other.[27] Ibn Qudama went even further by writing that the sole donor's want of knowledge invalidates the donation whereas the sole donee's want of knowledge does not. Donation of what is non-existent, or what cannot be delivered, such as an escaped animal or fish in the sea or bird in the air is not valid.[28]

22 For a complete study of the subject see Sadiq al-Darir's *al-Gharar wa atharuhu fi 'l-'uqud*, pp. 521ff., 1967.
23 Ibn Rushd, *Bidayat al-mujtahid*, Vol. II, p. 329.
24 Atfish, *Sharh al-Nil wa shifa' al-'alil*, Vol. VI, pp. 8 and 13; al-Shammakhi, *al-Idah*, Vol. IV, p. 408.
25 al-Shirazi, *al-Muhadhdhab*, Vol. I, p. 452; al-Shirbini, *Mughni al-muhtaj*, Vol. II, p. 399.
26 Ibn 'Abidin, *Radd al-muhtar*, Vol. IV, pp. 675 and 705.
27 al-Bahuti, *Kashshaf al-qina'*, Vol. IV, pp. 252, 257 and 258.
28 Ibn Qudama, *al-Mughni*, Vol. V, p. 657.

Wills

For the four Sunni schools,[29] a will is valid despite the fact that its subject-matter is non-existent, undetermined or outside the control of the testator and/or beneficiary.

The Ibadis legitimate a will whose subject-matter is unknown, provided the want of knowledge is not absolute.[30] What is non-existent, such as a coming crop, can be validly disposed of by a will according to some but not all Ibadi authors.[31] What is outside the control of the testator and/or beneficiary, such as an escaped animal, cannot be the subject-matter of a will.[32]

Power of attorney

The authority conferred by a power of attorney may be limited to one transaction or it may be general and unlimited. The impact of *gharar* on both types of power of attorney varies from one school of law to another as the following summaries illustrate.

Hanafis. A general power of attorney is valid in the eyes of the Hanafi scholars but there is controversy among them about the powers it confers on the agent. Some jurists have confined such powers to bilateral contracts where a consideration is involved, whereas others have broadened them to include nearly all secular transactions with the exception of repudiation (Islamic divorce, *talaq*), manumission (*ʿitq*), and setting up a pious foundation (*waqf*). As for limited powers of attorney such as entrusting an agent with the authority to buy an object, that object should be determined in a way which dispels any excessive (*fahish*) or even moderate (*mutawassit*) *gharar*, whereas an immaterial (*yasir*) *gharar* is tolerated.[33]

Malikis. The Maliki view on this matter is more lenient: a general power of attorney confers on the agent the authority to perform all kinds of advantageous secular transactions. Risky transactions can be conducted by the agent on behalf of the principal with a specific authorization; such authorization is also needed in the following cases: (a) divorcing the principal's wife, (b) consenting to the marriage of his eldest daughter, (c) disposing of his

29 Ibn ʿAbidin, *Radd al-muhtar*, Vol. v, pp. 570, 573, 588, 608 and 609; al-Dasuqi, *Commentaries of al-Sharh al-kabir. . . Dardir*, Vol. iv, pp. 433, 439, 440 and 447; al-Shafiʿi, *al-Umm*, Vol. iv, p. 90; al-Shirazi, *al-Muhadhdhab*, Vol. i, p. 458; Ibn Qudama, *al-Mughni*, Vol. vi, pp. 29–32, 56–59, 64 and 148–50.

30 Atfish, *Sharh al-Nil*, Vol. vi, pp. 189–90; al-Salimi, *Jawhar al-nizam*, Vol. iii, pp. 90–3.

31 In favour: al-Salimi, *Jawhar al-nizam* Vol. ii, p. 90; contra: Atfish, *Sharh al-Nil*, Vol. vi, p. 192.

32 Atfish, *Sharh al-Nil*, Vol. vi, p. 234.

33 Ibn ʿAbidin, *Radd al-muhtar*, Vol. iv, pp. 554–8.

dwelling-place and (d) disposing of the slave who is in charge of his affairs. Prevailing custom must direct the agent how to discharge his duty as it will also define the scope of a limited power of attorney which is impaired by sufficient want of knowledge to produce *gharar*.[34]

Shafiis. A general power of attorney is not valid, in the Shafii assessment, because of the material *gharar* it introduces. The subject of a limited power of attorney ought to be clearly defined. If the power of attorney is intended, for example, for buying an article, the species (*naw*ʿ) to which that article belongs is to be indicated, and if that is not enough for a proper identification, its class (*sanf*) and sub-class, if necessary, should be designated. If the power of attorney is intended for selling *all* the principal's belongings, that is valid even though those belongings are not named; but it is unlawful to say, for example, that the agent has authority to sell *some* of the principal's belongings without specifying which, for this amounts to *gharar* in the eyes of the Shafiis.[35]

Hanbalis. Hanbalis do not allow general powers of attorney, owing to the material *gharar* which such powers involve, according to their assessment. But a power of attorney limited to a designated category of acts can be performed with the fullest powers. Accordingly it is not valid to grant an agent authority to perform all kinds of transactions and operations on behalf of the principal, but it is valid to entrust him with the fullest authority to (for example) sell all the principal's belongings or to claim all the principal's rights. The power of attorney intended for buying an article is valid provided that the species to which that article belongs and also its price are known.[36]

Ibadis. Finally, the Ibadis term a general power of attorney *khilafa* and deem it valid. That is the case when the agent represents the principal in everything (*fi kull shay*'). As for a limited power of attorney, its subject ought to be defined, although some degree of want of knowledge is tolerated: such is the case when the agent is empowered to sell at his choice one or two camels of the principal's herd even though the sale price is not determined beforehand. However, the lack of a designated price was regarded with suspicion by some Ibadi jurists for the reason that this, added to the other degree of want of knowledge, i.e. the uncertainty about the subject-matter, would impair the operation with a material degree of *gharar*.[37]

[34] al-Dasuqi, *Commentaries*, Vol. III, p. 384.
[35] al-Shirbini, *Mughni al-muhtaj*, Vol. II, p. 223.
[36] al-Bahuti, *Sharh muntaha*, Vol. II, p. 303; al-Bahuti, *Kashshaf al-qina*ʿ, Vol. III, p. 482.
[37] Atfish, *Sharh al-Nil*, Vol. IV, pp. 693, 709 and 712.

To sum up, it can be said that as a matter of principle the subject-matter of a bilateral contract must be in existence, at least in its essence, at the time such a contract is concluded, otherwise the contract is void. This rules applies where the subject-matter is an object *in rem*. If, on the other hand, the subject-matter is work or use, this subject-matter is necessarily non-existent at the time the contract is concluded but materializes progressively with the gradual implementation of the contract. Despite this initial non-existence of the subject-matter, contracts of hire, lease and the like have always been tolerated by Islamic jurisprudence provided the use and the fee are determined in a way which dispels material *gharar*. As regards *gharar* in gratuitous contracts and unilateral transactions, all schools of law, with probably the sole exception of the Maliki one, see it as more or less an impairing factor but to a lesser degree than in bilateral contracts involving price or fee.

Islamic law, as already indicated briefly, has none the less tolerated a few types of contracts whose subject-matters are objects *in rem*, yet non-existent at the time of concluding such contracts. These are the sale of fruits and agricultural products, the contract of manufacture (*istisnaʿ*) and to a certain extent *bayʿ salam*. Investigation into these types of contracts and other related transactions will throw more light on the notion of *gharar*. The first two categories are reviewed immediately below, whereas *bayʿ salam* is examined later in this chapter, in section 4.

Sale of fruits and agricultural products

Nearly all Muslim scholars are in agreement that the sale of fruits or agricultural products which have not yet ripened is unlawful[38] with the exception that only the Malikis[39] and perhaps a very few of the Hanafis[40] allow the sale of fruits or agricultural products which ripen in succession during one harvest, if such sale accompanies the sale of what has already ripened. All Muslim scholars are in agreement about the lawfulness of the sale of fruits and agricultural products after they have been collected from trees or picked up from the field. Disagreement occurs, however, over the sale of fruits or agricultural products which have already ripened but have not yet been collected from trees or the field. The reason for this disagreement lies probably in the fact that, although all schools of law are aware that the motive behind the prohibition on selling fruits or agricultural products which are not yet harvested stems from the fear that they might be destroyed or suffer a defect before the buyer takes possession thereof, thus making the

[38] Ibn Rushd, *Bidayat al-mujtahid*, Vol. II, p. 149.
[39] Ibid., p. 157; Ibn Juzay, *Qawanin*, p. 287.
[40] Sanhuri, *Masadir al-haqq*, Vol. III, pp. 25ff.

transaction subject to arbitration, these schools of law disagree on the point where such fear ceases to be a legitimate one.

Generally speaking, schools of law concur in considering that the sale of fruits or agricultural products cannot be lawful except when the signs of readiness (*badu al-salah*) are shown, which means that the object of the sale is existent and free from defect, but they disagree on interpretation of "signs of readiness". For the Malikis,[41] Shafiis,[42] Hanbalis[43] and Ibadis, in their more favoured opinion,[44] fruits and agricultural products indicate signs of readiness when showing signs of ripeness or sweetness. The Hanafis have apparently a different view: for them, fruits and agricultural products indicate signs of readiness when they are no longer at the flowering stage but have attained their final appearance.[45] Once this appearance is reached, fruits and agricultural products may be sold, even before they show signs of ripeness or sweetness. Furthermore, the Hanafis alone among the other schools of law consider that the sale of fruits and agricultural products with the *implicit* condition that they should remain on trees or in the field until they ripen is valid, but if the requisite is made an *explicit* one then the sale becomes void.[46] For the other Sunni schools of law and the Ibadis, the sale of fruits and agricultural products which are left on trees or in the field is unlawful even if it is made with no condition at all, except in the case where fruits or agricultural products are sold together with the principal, i.e. the tree or the field, in one transaction.[47] The Ibadis seem also to allow the sale of ripe fruits or mature agricultural products with the condition that they should remain on the trees or in the field for a specific period of time.[48]

Finally, only the Malikis, among Sunni schools and among Ibadis, validate the sale of agricultural products which are buried in the earth, such as carrots, onions, garlic and radish;[49] and Shafiis alone prohibit the sale of fruits or other agricultural products still in their natural external envelope such as nuts in the shell or grains in the ear, provided that this envelope can be removed without hastening the decomposition of the fruit or other agricultural products – which is not the case with eggs, for example.[50]

41 Ibn Juzay, *Qawanin*, p. 287.
42 al-Shirazi, *al-Muhadhdhab*, Vol. I, p. 281.
43 Ibn Qudama, *al-Mughni*, Vol. IV, pp. 92ff.
44 al-Shammakhi, *al-Idah*, Vol. III, pp. 57ff.
45 Mahmasani, *The General Theory*, Vol. II, p. 329.
46 Sanhuri, *Masadir al-haqq*, Vol. III, pp. 17–18.
47 Ibn Qudama, *al-Mughni*, Vol. IV, pp. 96–7; Ibn Rushd, *Bidayat al-mujtahid*, Vol. II, p. 150; al-Shafiʿi, *al-Umm*, Vol. III, p. 43; al-Shammakhi, *al-Idah*, Vol. III, p. 59 (note) and p. 60.
48 al-Shammakhi, *al-Idah*, Vol. III, p. 64; al-Basyani, *Mukhtasar*, p. 306.
49 Ibn Rushd, *Bidayat al-mujtahid*, Vol. II, p. 157; Ibn Qudama, *al-Mughni*, Vol. IV, pp. 104–5; al-Kasani, *Badaʾiʿ*, Vol. V, p. 139; al-Shafiʿi, *al-Umm*, Vol. III, p. 51; al-Shammakhi, *al-Idah*, Vol. III, pp. 66–7.
50 Ibn Qudama, *al-Mughni*, Vol. IV, pp. 104–5; al-Shafiʿi, *al-Umm*, Vol. III, pp. 50, 51, 61.

*Istisna*ʿ (contract of manufacture)

*Istisna*ʿ is the giving of an order to a labourer or artisan to make a definite article with agreement to pay a definite price for that article when made; an example is when an order is passed to a shoemaker to make a pair of shoes for a price fixed in advance.[51] This price is to be paid only when the pair of shoes is ready for delivery. The unsatisfactory aspects of the contract of manufacture are obvious, for nothing changes hands immediately, and not only is the subject-matter non-existent at the time the contract is concluded but also payment of the price is deferred. Yet remarkably enough, *fiqh* admitted the validity of the *istisna*ʿ transaction on the grounds of a custom which has prevailed from the time of the Prophet himself and justified it by the necessities of business[52] and by equity (*istihsan*). The exact nature of the contract of manufacture is disputed: it was considered by some authors as a hire contract, by others as a sale contract and by a third group as having features of both.[53] Whatever is the nature of the contract of manufacture (*istisna*ʿ) its subject-matter should be well defined, leaving no room for uncertainty or ambiguity with respect either to the quality or to the quantity of goods involved. The price should likewise be well determined,[54] although payment to the manufacturer is postponed until the ordered article is delivered. However, there is a material discrepancy between the Islamic schools of law with regard to the binding effect of *istisna*ʿ.

For Abu Hanifa the contract of manufacture (*istisna*ʿ), although assimilated to a sale contract, is not binding, at least initially, upon either the client or the manufacturer. This initial stage is between the time of giving the order and the time the client sees the manufactured object. During that time the manufacturer may, if he so wishes, refrain from manufacturing the ordered article and equally the client may cancel his order. Once the article is manufactured and shown to the client, the latter (though the manufacturer has no right to cancel the contract), always, according to Abu Hanifa, has the option of rejecting it without further responsibility. This is probably because Hanafi teaching gives such a predominant role to the concept of the "option after inspection" (*khiyar al-ru'ya*).[55] However, Abu Yusuf, the brilliant disciple of Abu Hanifa, denies to the manufacturer the right to

[51] al-Kasani, *Bada'i*ʿ, Vol. v, p. 2.
[52] Abdur Rahim, *Muhammadan Jurisprudence*, p. 293.
[53] Ibid.
[54] Sanhuri, *Masadir al-haqq*, Vol. III, p. 38.
[55] Ibid., p. 39. It is generally taught that the right of option (*haqq al-khiyar*) is of three kinds, namely the option after inspection (*khiyar al-ru'ya*, which is the purchaser's option of rejecting the object of the sale after sight; the option determined by the quality (*khiyar al-wasf*), which means that either of the parties may cancel the contract on discovery that the quality he required is not provided; and the option on discovery of a defect (*khiyar al-*ʿ*ayb*) which is the option of dissolving the contract if the goods are discovered to be defective.

refrain from manufacturing the ordered article as he equally denies to the client the right to reject it once it is manufactured according to the order.[56] In other words, the contract of manufacture (*istisnaʿ*) is for Abu Yusuf a binding one from the outset.

For the other schools of law also, *istisnaʿ* is binding;[57] therefore if there is a dispute between the client and the manufacturer with respect to the characteristics of the manufactured article, the presumption is in favour of the manufacturer, provided he takes an oath, according to Hanbalis,[58] Malikis[59] and Ibadis.[60] As for the Shafiis it seems that despite a disparity in their teaching with regard to this particular problem, they are in favour of the solution whereby both manufacturer and client take the oath.[61] When the dispute between manufacturer and the client relates to the price of the manufactured article, schools of law hold the following views. Manufacturer and client should both take the oath, according to Hanbalis and Shafiis,[62] whether or not the article is already manufactured; if oaths are contradictory, the contract is rescinded. Hanafis hold the same view for the situation, when the article is not yet manufactured; but once it has been manufactured, then the manufacturer is to be believed, provided he takes the oath.[63] For the Malikis, the manufacturer is also to be believed when the order is in the recent past, otherwise the client's word is taken into consideration.[64] Ibadis put the burden of proof on the client, otherwise the manufacturer is entitled to obtain a fair price.[65]

The price

The price in a sale contract, likewise the subject-matter, should be in existence at the time the contract is concluded, otherwise the contract is void. When this price is a property (*mal*) which is not currency, then the previously described rules intended for the subject-matter apply. When the price is currency, it should be in circulation (*mutadawal*) and its species and quantum should be well specified, as will be examined in more detail in the course of studying credit sale (see below, pp. 65ff.). If figures and kinds of coins are indicated but not the features of the coins,[66] such as "ten dinars"

56 Ibid.
57 Ibn Qudama, *al-Mughni*, Vol. v, p. 448.
58 Ibn Qudama, *al-Mughni*, Vol. v, p. 531.
59 Ibn Juzay, *Qawanin*, p. 305; Ibn Rushd, *Bidayat al-mujtahid*, Vol. II, p. 233.
60 al-Basyani, *Mukhtasar*, p. 287.
61 al-Shafiʿi, *al-Umm*, Vol. IV, pp. 39–40; Ibn Qudama, *al-Mughni*, Vol. v, p. 531.
62 Ibn Qudama, *al-Mughni*, Vol. v, p. 559; al-Shafiʿi, *al-Umm*, Vol. IV, p. 39.
63 Ibid.
64 Ibn Rushd, *Bidayat al-mujtahid*, Vol. II, p. 234.
65 al-Basyani, *Mukhtasar*, p. 288.
66 The weight standard and the alloy of the dinar was maintained in most parts of the Islamic world for some time; however, by the time the above questions were discussed by Muslim

with no other specifications, Hanafis,[67] Malikis[68] and Shafiis[69] teach that the type of dinar most frequently circulating in the country where the sale was concluded is to be retained. The Hanbalis on the other hand advocate that the average currency is the one to be chosen.[70] When, in a given country, different currencies have the same value and the same degree of circulation, a sale contract which fails to indicate the characteristics of the coins representing the price is still valid, and the purchaser is entitled to settle the price in any of the circulating coins, according to Hanafis[71] and some Malikis.[72] This is not the view of the Hanbalis[73] and some other Malikis[74] who teach that the sale contract would be invalid unless the parties agree on the disputed issue; nor is it the view of the Shafiis,[75] who teach that the magistrate is the one to determine the kind of coins with which payment should be made.

4 Avoiding want of knowledge (*jahl*) concerning the characteristics and quantities of the exchanged countervalues, and the date of future performance

Islamic *fiqh* has persistently emphasized that the exchanged countervalues in a bilateral transaction should be in existence at the time such a transaction is concluded. This is basically because the contracting parties ought to be in a position to inspect and examine them, to be acquainted with their characteristics and aware of the quantum involved; all these are prerequisites to taking the decision to enter into the agreement. In other words, no material want of knowledge (*jahl*) should subsist with regard to the exchanged countervalues, otherwise *riba* or *gharar*, or both, have a greater chance to infiltrate the transaction contemplated by the contracting parties: and *riba* and *gharar* are, in the eyes of Islamic law, two evils which should be averted at all cost in secular transactions (*muʿamalat*).

The safest way to avoid *riba* and *gharar* would be to have the exchanged countervalues in hand, to inspect them and decide on whether or not to enter the proposed transaction. In this manner uncertainty is dispelled and *riba* is surely avoided: properties susceptible of *riba al-fadl* (*riba* by way of excess)

scholars, specimens of coins showed great irregularity in both weight and fineness, differed from place to place and received different appellations (J. Wakin, *The Function of Documents in Islamic Law*, pp. 86–7).

67 Sanhuri, *Masadir al-haqq*, Vol. III, pp. 75–7; Ibn al Himam, *Fath al-qadir*, Vol. V, pp. 84–5.
68 al-Kashnawi, *Ashal al-madarik*, Vol. II, p. 266.
69 al-Nawawi, *al-Majmuʿ*, Vol. IX, p. 329.
70 Ibn Qudama, *al-Mughni*, Vol. IV, p. 217.
71 Sanhuri, *Masadir al-haqq*, Vol. III, pp. 75–7.
72 al-Hattab, *Mawahib al-jalil*, Vol. IV, p. 278.
73 Ibn Qudama, *al-Mughni*, Vol. IV, p. 217.
74 al-Kashnawi, *Ashal al-madarik*, Vol. II, p. 266.
75 al-Nawawi, *al-Majmuʿ*, Vol. IX, p. 329.

will not be exchanged except in a hand-to-hand transaction and in scrupulously exact quantities, and properties susceptible of *riba al-nasi'a* (*riba* by way of deferment) will not be exchanged except in a hand-to-hand transaction.[76]

The actual presence of the subject-matter and knowledge of the price at the meeting of the contracting parties dispels all elements of uncertainty or speculation, which means that neither of the contracting parties is assuming a risk with respect to the identification of the subject-matter or the price. This is not to say that commercial risk is unlawful under Islamic law; on the contrary, commercial ventures and commerce in general are activities welcomed by Islamic society and looked upon sympathetically by Islamic law. The risk which *is* disallowed is that involving the identification of the subject-matter and the price, because when uncertainty obscures either the subject-matter or the price, the perils of *riba* and *gharar* are greater, and thus injustice and inequity have, from the outset, a greater chance to fall on the ill-advised contracting party or parties. In other words, Sharia concedes risk from "the without" i.e. risk generated by financial and commercial factors and elements extrinsic to the formation of the transaction, namely "business risk", whereas risk from "the within" i.e. risk accompanying the inception of the transaction is penalized. Contracting parties are allowed to expose themselves to the outer risk of a given venture provided that when they engage in such a venture they are equipped with the advance knowledge of the elements which constitute that venture.

To require the presence of the subject-matter and the payment at the meeting of the contracting parties is undoubtedly the safest way of dispelling the perils of *riba* and *gharar*; nevertheless it is often an impracticable requirement. Sometimes the sale object is available at the meeting of the contracting parties but not the payment, sometimes it is the payment which is at hand but not the subject-matter. It can also happen that the subject-matter or the payment is available at the meeting of the contracting parties but in an undetermined quantity. Business in its infinite varieties could not be defeated by theoretical thinking, so a solution had to be found.

In a fairly advanced merchant society such as the one encountered in the Hijaz during the Prophet's time and especially during the later Arab Empire, people continued to exchange what they did not have in hand, what they did not see and even what they did not own. Business contingencies and legal requirements were about to clash. Islamic jurisprudence yielded to the pressure and learned men endeavoured to formulate permissible exceptions to the rule. Sale of a subject-matter unapparent at the meeting of the parties, but where title is held by the vendor, became known as *bay' gha'ib* and sale where the vendor is not in possession of the sale object but undertakes to make it available was known as *bay' salam*. Credit sale became more strongly

[76] For more detail on *riba* see above, pp. 12ff.

established than ever and, most amazingly, a kind of sale where sometimes the subject-matter and sometimes the price was not precisely defined (*bayʿ juzaf*) was recognized as a valid transaction under specific conditions. All these kinds of sale and other related transactions will now be examined.

Payment unavailable at the parties' meeting

One of the reasons for the non-availability of the payment at the meeting of the contracting parties occurs when the performed transaction is a credit sale. Credit sale is the contract of sale in which credit is given for the whole or a material part of the price. Property in the articles which are the subject of the sale passes at once to the buyer, the seller being only a personal creditor for the unpaid price. This is in contrast with *bay' salam*, where payment of the price is made forthwith, despite the fact that the object of the sale is to be delivered at a later stage. In a credit sale where the price is represented by currency, the exchange of the two countervalues can be deferred with or without gain, even though the object of the sale is a property susceptible of *riba* (*mal ribawi*), provided such an object is not currency. (For if both countervalues were currencies the transaction would amount to an exchange – *sarf* – and as such would have to obey different rules.) We have seen earlier, in the course of our study of *riba*, that Shafiis and Hanbalis explain that permissive attitude on the basis that since *bayʿ salam* is allowed, so should credit sale be. Hanafis for their part have divided weighable articles (currency was one of them) into two different categories: on the one hand currency, i.e. gold and silver weighable on a highly precise scale, and on the other hand all other weighable articles whose weight is obtained by the use of a normal scale. The two categories are not deemed to share the same weighable quality (which is a Hanafi *ʿilla*) and thus the sale of a weighable article susceptible of *riba* for a deferred payment in currency or for a deferred delivery is also lawful.

The Maliki school of law, which more than any other Sunni school recognizes the validity of a deferred transaction, considers credit sale as a valid and lawful transaction whether or not the price is inflated provided it is not used as a stratagem or device in order to circumvent the prohibition of *riba* as is the case when an apparent credit sale is, in reality, a cover for a loan agreement – with the lender having secured for himself some advantage from the loan.[77] This limitation is also shared by the Hanbalis.

Ibadis, as seen in the course of studying *riba*, take a favourable view of credit sale with or without an increase in the price and whether or not the property which is the subject of the sale is susceptible of *riba* (*mal ribawi*), provided that the price is currency and the object of the sale is not; that is to say, provided it is not an exchange (*sarf*).

77 Ibn Juzay, *Qawanin*, p. 297.

The situation is different when in a credit sale the two exchanged countervalues are properties *in rem* either or both of them susceptible of *riba* (*mal ribawi*). In such a case principles and rules set forth in order to avert *riba al-nasi'a* (*riba* by way of deferment) should receive full application. These principles and rules vary from one school of law to the other and can be examined in detail on pp. 19ff. above.

It may happen that the payment of the price is deferred not because credit is given to the purchaser but for the reason that the price is not determined during the meetings of the contracting parties (*majlis al-ʿaqd*) and is to be determined afterwards. This is unacceptable by Sharia standards. Even when the price is to be determined either by a decision to be taken by a given person or by reference to market price or by analogy with a sale performed by a third party, Islamic schools of law, with perhaps a slight exception advocated by the Hanbali school, as we will soon see, resist such practices on the ground that these sales entail *gharar*. *Gharar* can be dispelled only by the determination of the price during the meeting of the vendor and purchaser whether or not such a price is to be disbursed forthwith or at a later stage.[78] For instance, Hanafis consider the sale of a slave at his market value or for a price to be fixed by a third party or by the purchaser himself as being unlawful.[79] For the Shafiis a sale with an unfixed price or a price to be determined by the purchaser is invalid; nevertheless a sale for a price indicated on the article proposed for sale or for a price similar to the one for which a sale transaction was concluded is lawful, provided the contracting parties know the price to which they refer. If only one of the contracting parties knows such a price, there are conflicting views on the validity of the transaction; the prevailing tendency is to bar it on the ground of *gharar*.[80] In the Maliki view the price is subject to want of knowledge (*jahl*), causing *gharar*, when it is to be determined according to today's price or to market price or by a decision to be taken by a given person.[81]

Hanbalis stress that the price, being one of the two countervalues, should be known in the same way as the object of the sale.[82] Sale with reference to the price normally paid is invalid, owing to the uncertainty it imports.[83] More flexibility however, is shown in other circumstances; thus the sale either for the price affixed on the proposed article or for a price similar to the one for which a given person concluded a transaction is valid, not only when the two contracting persons are aware of the referred price but also, apparently, when only one of them is aware of the price.[84]

[78] al-Salimi, *Jawhar al-nizam*, p. 331, 1344 A.H. edn.
[79] al-Kasani, *Bada'iʿ*, Vol. v, p. 157.
[80] al-Nawawi, *al-Majmuʿ*, Vol. IX, pp. 332–3.
[81] Ibn Juzay, *Qawanin*, pp. 282–3.
[82] al-Bahuti, *Kashshaf al-qinaʿ*, Vol. III, p. 162.
[83] Ibid., p. 193.
[84] al-Bahuti, *Kashshaf al-qinaʿ*, Vol. III, p. 193; Ibn Qudama, *al-Mughni*, Vol. IV, p. 207.

The aversion to transactions which involve an element of risk or speculation has led to the virtual unanimity of Islamic schools of law in forbidding the practice of paying earnest money, understood in the sense of a sum of money given by the potential purchaser to the potential seller as a portion of the total price in the event that the transaction is concluded and as a lump-sum compensation in the event that the potential purchaser changes his mind and decides not to finalize the contract.[85] Only Hanbalis do not condemn the practice of earnest money.[86]

For all Islamic schools of law, a term in a credit sale giving time for payment should be defined,[87] leaving no room for uncertainty. A coming harvest or non-Muslim festivals are not valid periods for payment in the eyes of the Shafiis, Hanafis and most Hanbalis, on the ground of uncertainty in the former case and, in the latter one, on the ground that Muslims are not bound to know the exact date of festivals celebrated by religious communities which have a calendar different from the Muslim one.[88] Malikis and a Hanbali view reported on Ibn Hanbal's part do not see such dates as being uncertain.[89] As for the Ibadis, they hold conflicting views on the matter, with a strong trend towards considering such dates as uncertain,[90] as did the Shafiis and Hanafis.

Subject-matter unavailable at the parties' meeting
(I) *bayʿ gha'ib*

Bayʿ gha'ib is sale of what is not visible at the meeting of the parties. The vendor in a *bayʿ gha'ib* has title over the subject-matter, but that subject-matter is not apparent at the meeting of the contracting parties; for either it is elsewhere, or it is present but out of sight, or at least out of the potential purchaser's sight. Islamic schools of law have different approaches in their assessment of *bayʿ gha'ib* in its dual aspects. Their views range from the prohibition of selling what has not been actually inspected by the potential purchaser, as the Shafiis hold, to the lawfulness of a sale concluded by either the vendor pointing out the place where the subject-matter is hidden or by the vendor describing the subject-matter, as the Hanafis hold. The conflicting views of the different schools of law stem most probably from their disagreement over what is called *khiyar al-ru'ya* or the "option after inspection", which means that the purchaser enjoys the option of rejecting

[85] Hanafis, Malikis, Shafiis and Ibadis disallow the practice of earnest money, called in Arabic *ʿirban* or *ʿurbun* (Ibn Rushd, *Bidayat al-mujtahid*, Vol. II, pp. 162–3; Ibn Qudama, *al-Mughni*, Vol. IV, p. 257; al-Shammakhi, *al-Idah*, Vol. III, p. 80).

[86] Ibn Qudama, *al-Mughni*, Vol. IV, p. 256.

[87] Ibn Rushd, *Bidayat al-mujtahid*, Vol. II, p. 172; al-Shammakhi, *al-Idah*, Vol. III, p. 70.

[88] al-Shafiʿi, *al-Umm*, Vol. III, p. 96; Damad Effendi, *Majmaʿ al-anhur*, Vol. II, pp. 63–4; Ibn Qudama, *al-Mughni*, Vol. IV, pp. 322 ff.

[89] al-Nawawi, *al-Majmaʿ*, Vol. IX, p. 340; Ibn Qudama, *al-Mughni*, Vol. IV, p. 322.

[90] al-Shammakhi, *al-Idah*, Vol. III, pp. 368–9.

the object of the sale after sight and consequently of rescinding the sale. The Shafiis do not acknowledge that a purchaser has the "option after inspection" (*khiyar al-ru'ya*), and consequently the purchaser in this case ought to be very careful and aware of what he is buying before entering a sale contract. The Hanafis, on the contrary, were in a position to lay down less stringent conditions for the conclusion of a *bayʿ gha'ib*, for the reason that the buyer in their view always has the right to repudiate the sale once he is in a position to inspect the object of the sale. Moreover, Hanafis, contrary to Malikis and Hanbalis (who none the less acknowledge the legality of the purchaser's "option after inspection" but with more restrictive effects than the Hanafis), do not deprive the purchaser of the "option after inspection" even when the object of sale is in perfect conformity with the description which induced the purchaser to enter a sale of contract. This limited specimen of the differences found in the views of the schools of law with respect to *bayʿ gha'ib* prompts a closer investigation of this kind of sale.

Shafiis. According to their widely accepted teaching, they regard as invalid the sale of what is invisible at the meeting of the contracting parties (*majlis al-ʿaqd*) owing to the *gharar* it involves,[91] whether the subject-matter is actually not present at the meeting of the contracting parties or, on the contrary, present at their meeting but out of their sight or at least out of the sight of the prospective buyer.[92] However, it is not a requisite that the object of the sale be inspected at the very moment the contract is concluded. A prior inspection is sufficient, provided that the object is of a kind which does not necessarily undergo a change between the date of inspection and the date when the contract is concluded; an example of such a valid sale would be that of a piece of land or the sale of iron or copper.[93] Moreover, it is not necessary that the prospective purchaser sees all the subject-matter if seeing part of it gives an indication of the remaining parts; this presupposes that all the subject-matter's parts are alike. For example, when the prospective buyer examines a measure of wheat he can validly buy the remaining wheat of the same quality. In this manner a sale according to sample or specimen is allowed, provided it obeys the same rules.[94] On the contrary, the inspection of a house from the outside does not dispense with the necessity for inspection of the interior, for the reason that the outside is not indicative of the inside.[95]

Hanafis. They have a more liberal view on *bayʿ gha'ib* because, as already seen, of their interpretation of the technique of the "option after inspection" (*khiyar al-ru'ya*), which successfully reduces the risk inherent in an imperfect knowledge of the subject-matter. For the Hanafis it is valid to sell

[91] al-Nawawi, *al-Majmuʿ*, Vol. IX, p. 301.
[92] Jaziri, *al-Fiqh ʿala al-madhahib*, Vol. II, p. 214.
[93] Ibid., p. 215. [94] Ibid. [95] Ibid., p. 216.

an object by pointing out its location, so as to dispel a material want of knowledge (*jahl*). Such is the case when the vendor announces: "I sell to you the animal which is in my sleeve", or "I sell to you an object which is in this box."[96] When the object of the sale is not present at the meeting of the parties, the vendor ought to particularize it by indicating the place where it is located, for example by saying: "I have sold to you the animal which is in such a place", provided that the vendor has no other animal in that place. Otherwise the vendor ought to describe the subject-matter in such a way as to dispel a material want of knowledge; an immaterial want of knowledge does not invalidate the contract, which is anyway controlled by the technique of *khiyar al-ru'ya* – this is open to the purchaser even though not stipulated as a sale requisite[97] and even though the subject-matter turns out to be in conformity with the description.[98] However, once the buyer has seen the subject-matter he is thereby precluded from exercising the "option after inspection", for that option is open only to the buyer who has not inspected the object of the sale by the time the contract is concluded. Seeing part of the subject-matter which is indicative of the remaining parts, when all the subject-matter's parts are alike, is sufficient to deprive the buyer of the "option after inspection", therefore sale according to sample or specimen is binding and not subject to *khiyar al-ru'ya*.[99]

Malikis. When the object of the sale is available at the meeting of the parties, Malikis are of the opinion that no valid sale can take place unless the purchaser has laid eyes on it (*bi'l-ru'ya*). If the object of the sale is not present, or if present not apparent, then it can be sold according to description[100] or even, in place of description with the "option after inspection",[101] as one isolated Maliki opinion teaches.[102] In any event, when the sale *is* performed according to description it cannot be accompanied by the "option after inspection" (*khiyar al-ru'ya*) for, contrary to the Hanafis, the Malikis do not combine description and "option after inspection"; either an article is sold according to description, or with no description but with the "option after inspection". When a sale is concluded according to description and when the object of the sale is in conformity with the description, the sale is binding; this is contrary to the Hanafis, who allow the buyer to repudiate the sale even though the object of the sale perfectly matches its description.[103] Inspecting the subject-matter before the date of concluding the sale contract is valid, provided that such subject-matter is not

[96] Sanhuri, *Masadir al-haqq*, Vol. III, p. 63.
[97] Jaziri, *al-Fiqh 'ala al-madhahib*, Vol. II, p. 217.
[98] al-Nawawi, *al-Majmu'*, Vol. IX, p. 301.
[99] Jaziri, *al-Fiqh 'ala al-madhahib*, Vol. II, p. 219.
[100] al-Hattab, *Mawahib al-jalil*, Vol. IV, pp. 285–6.
[101] Sanhuri, *Masadir al-haqq*, Vol. III, p. 63.
[102] Ibn Rushd, *Bidayat al-mujtahid*, Vol. II, pp. 155–6.
[103] Ibid., p. 155.

in a remote place so as to undergo a change between inspection date and closing date.[104] Fungible articles, i.e. those that are measurable or weighable or accounted by number when alike, can be sold according to sample or according to a descriptive *pro forma* (*barnamij*).[105]

Hanbalis. They allow *bayʿ gha'ib* under two conditions: first the subject-matter should be of a kind which can be sold *bayʿ salam* (see below) i.e. it should be a weighable or measurable article such as wheat or a piece of land or articles which can be described precisely (precious stones are not included in this category nor is jewellery); secondly the subject-matter should be described in a way which enables its precise identification, such as is the case when the vendor tells the purchaser: "I have sold to you such a quantity of small red Zaghluli dates."[106] When the object of the sale is in conformity with the description or even better than the description, the purchaser is not in a position to rescind the contract.[107] Sale with prior inspection of the subject-matter is lawful, provided that the object of the sale is not of a kind which necessarily undergoes a change between inspection date and closing date.[108] Sale according to sample or specimen is not lawful, for the purchaser has not seen the actual subject-matter;[109] on the other hand when the purchaser has seen one element of the subject-matter, and that is indicative of the remaining similar elements, that is acceptable and sale is lawful.[110]

Ibadis. In the course of his analysis of *bayʿ gha'ib*, the Ibadi author al-Shammakhi examined different teachings of various schools of law with respect to *bayʿ gha'ib* and indicated the one which he favoured and which is close to the Hanafi view. This holds that a sale according to description is lawful provided the purchaser can always exercise the option of rejecting the object of the sale after sight, whether or not such an object turns out to be in conformity with the description, provided that at least the vendor has knowledge of the object of the sale, because otherwise the transaction would involve a strong element of *gharar*.[111] Sale with prior inspection is valid provided the object of the sale has not undergone a change between inspection date and closing date;[112] if in the mean time a change has occurred, the sale can be cancelled.[113] Sale of an animal is lawful only when

[104] Ibid., p. 156.
[105] Jaziri, *al-Fiqh ʿala al-madhahib*, Vol. II, p. 220.
[106] Ibid., p. 222. Zaghluli is a variety of date.
[107] Ibn Qudama, *al-Mughni*, Vol. IV, p. 171.
[108] Jaziri, *al-Fiqh ʿala al-madhahib*, Vol. II, p. 223.
[109] Ibid.
[110] Ibid.
[111] al-Shammakhi, *al-Idah*, Vol. III, p. 114.
[112] Ibid., pp. 115–16.
[113] al-Basyani, *Mukhtasar*, p. 179.

the animal is present at the meeting of the contracting parties;[114] in other words an animal cannot be the object of *bayʿ gha'ib*.

Subject-matter unavailable at the parties' meeting (2) *bayʿ salam*

Bayʿ salam is sale with advance payment for future delivery. In *bayʿ salam*, the vendor has no title over the sale object but undertakes to make it available to the purchaser. The subject-matter of *bayʿ salam* is a promise given against payment and not an object *in rem*; a personal obligation and not an object in kind. Under strict Sharia rules this kind of sale would be unlawful, for the vendor deals with an article which is not in his possession. Nevertheless, *bayʿ salam* was admitted by Sharia on the ground of a tradition attributed to the Prophet himself and on the ground of consensus (*ijmaʿ*) and because it responds to public needs. *Bayʿ salam*, being an exception to a general rule, namely that the sale object should be available to the contracting parties at the time the sale is concluded, is bound by special rules intended to minimize the danger of *gharar* and, rather theoretically, the danger of *riba*. In this connection the subject-matter and the price in a *bayʿ salam* cannot both be currencies, for the deferred exchange of currencies with or without an excess is unlawful according to nearly all schools of law. (However, the Ibadis seem to admit a deferred exchange of currencies when it occurs with no gain.)

With regard to *gharar*, and how to avert it, Ibn Qudama, the great Hanbali author, made a remarkable study of what he called *ʿilm* which means, in the present context, knowledge of the subject-matter. He said in substance that *ʿilm* is one of the sale's requisites; it is attained either by viewing the subject-matter or by having a description. In *salam* the viewing of the subject-matter is out of the question, so only description is possible. For a description to be acceptable, it should define the genus and species, and state whether the article, the object of *salam*, is in good or bad condition. Abu Hanifa and Malik, according to Ibn Qudama, are satisfied with that amount of description of the subject-matter which constitutes, in their view, sufficient means for the identification of the *salam* object, whereas Ibn Hanbal and Shafii require other defining characteristics, namely colour, country of origin and any other feature which has an effect on the price or on the use.[115] This is not the only point where the schools of law diverge on the subject of *salam*. Hence a proper assessment of this type of sale can only be achieved by a survey of the views of the main schools of law on this matter.

[114] Ibid.

[115] Ibn Qudama, *al-Mughni*, Vol. IV, pp. 310–11.

Hanafi *salam*. Articles either weighable or measurable or accounted by number, provided they are alike, or agricultural products, can be a *salam* object.[116] They should be normally available on the market and able to be defined by description.[117] Living animals cannot be *salam* objects and there is a controversy with respect to dead animals, with a trend towards disallowing *salam* whose subject-matter is a dead animal. The tendency is, however, to allow *salam* whose object is meat.[118] A characteristic of Hanafi *salam* is that the subject-matter of a *salam* ought to be in existence from the time the contract is concluded until the time of delivery.[119]

The price of a *salam* may be in money or in kind;[120] when it is in kind it should not have in common with the subject-matter one of the two elements forming the Hanafi *ʿilla*, namely (1) the fact that the exchanged countervalues belong to the same genus as interpreted by the Hanafis or (2) the property of being both weighable or both measurable when they change hands. Otherwise *riba al-nasiʾa* (*riba* by way of deferment) occurs, whether or not there is an excess in one of the exchanged countervalues.[121] Whether the price is in money or in kind it should be paid at the meeting of the parties.[122] But since *salam* is a deferred transaction, in that the delivery of the subject-matter has to be postponed, immediate delivery renders such a sale invalid in the Hanafi conception, which generally speaking has set as a requisite that a delay of at least one month is necessary.[123] Yet Ibn Rushd has attributed to Abu Hanifa a ruling that the minimum delay is three days.[124] If the vendor dies before the delay has elapsed, *salam* reaches maturity date[125] and the remainder of the delay is waived. The place of delivery of the *salam* object should be determined by the parties only if it entails extra expense.[126] The vendor's obligation in a *salam* can be secured by a pledge or a guarantee.[127]

Shafii *salam*. The subject-matter of *salam* ought to be of the kind available at the time of delivery, though not necessarily at the time the contract was concluded.[128] Any article determinable by description can be a *salam* object, even unlike articles accounted by number.[129] Domestic animals can be a *salam* object.[130]

116 Jaziri, *al-Fiqh ʿala al-madhahib*, Vol. II, p. 307.
117 Ibid., pp. 306–7. 118 Ibid., p. 308.
119 Sanhuri, *Masadir al-haqq*, Vol. III, p. 35.
120 Jaziri, *al-Fiqh ʿala al-madhahib*, Vol. II, p. 306.
121 Ibid., p. 307. 122 Ibid., p. 306.
123 Sanhuri, *Masadir al-haqq*, Vol. III, p. 35.
124 Ibn Rushd, *Bidayat al-mujtahid*, Vol. II, p. 203.
125 Ibid. – for what constitutes an established term giving time for performance in the eyes of the five schools of law under scrutiny, see p. 67 above.
126 Jaziri, *al-Fiqh ʿala al-madhahib*, Vol. II, p. 307.
127 al-Kasani, *Badaʾiʿ* Vol. IV, pp. 142–3.
128 Jaziri, *al-Fiqh ʿala al-madhahib*, Vol. II, p. 316; Sanhuri, *Masadir al-haqq*, Vol. III, p. 37.
129 Ibid., p. 38.
130 al-Muzni, *Mukhtasar*, p. 90.

Payment of the price must take place before the parties separate. It need not consist of currency and may even consist of the use of some object, but possession must be taken of the price before the parties leave.[131] This price and the *salam* object should not both be foodstuffs or both currencies, whether or not they belong to the same genus, otherwise *riba* by way of deferment (*riba al-nasi'a*) results.

In the Shafii view, *salam* can be immediate and not necessarily a postponed transaction;[132] thus there is no minimum delay prescribed for delivery. Immediate *salam* is a concept peculiar to the Shafii school of law; no other school of law seems to advocate it. The death of the vendor in a normal deferred *salam* brings about maturity date.[133] If the vendor provides the *salam* object before the agreed time, the purchaser may refuse to accept delivery if he has a valid reason for doing so, for example if this object is an animal and the purchaser would have to feed it, or if a hostile incursion is apprehended at the moment of the proposed delivery. If the purchaser cannot provide any good reason for his refusal he would have to accept early delivery, especially when the vendor himself has good reason for expediting delivery, for example if he wishes to redeem a pledge or if he simply wants to discharge his obligation.[134]

Whether *salam* is immediate or for future delivery, the place where the *salam* object should be delivered has to be indicated, in the case of the place where the contract was concluded being an unsuitable place of delivery. If this place is a suitable one and if moving the *salam* object to such a place necessitates expense, then all these details should be made clear in a *salam* for future delivery, but not in an immediate *salam*; if moving the *salam* object does not necessitate extra expense, then nothing needs to be stated on this, whether in a *salam* for future delivery or otherwise.[135] A binding obligation such as the vendor's obligation in a *salam* can be secured by a pledge[136] or a guarantee.

Maliki *salam*. That a *salam* object can be any weighable or measurable article is unanimously agreed by all the different scholars, as noted by Ibn Rushd.[137] Generally speaking, an article which can be identified by description can be a *salam* object; however, it is the implementation of this principle which is the object of a controversy. Thus, animals are a disputed issue; we have seen that Hanafis do not deem animals as a proper *salam* object; whereas Malikis have settled for the opposite.[138] According to Maliki

131 al-Nawawi, *Minhaj al-talibin*, p. 147 (trans. E. C. Howard).
132 Jaziri, *al-Fiqh 'ala al-madhahib*, Vol. II, p. 305.
133 Sanhuri, *Masadir al-haqq*, Vol. III, p. 38.
134 al-Nawawi, *Minhaj al-talibin*, p. 150.
135 Jaziri, *al-Fiqh 'ala al-madhahib*, Vol. II, p. 316.
136 al-Shirazi, *al-Muhadhdhab*, Vol. I, p. 312.
137 Ibn Rushd, *Bidayat al-mujtahid*, Vol. II, p. 201.
138 Ibid.

teaching it is not necessary that a *salam* object be available at the time the contract is concluded.[139]

Price may be in money or in kind.[140] When in kind, it should not have with the subject-matter the common quality of being foodstuffs, even when the price and the subject-matter belong to two different genera; the reason is to avert *riba al-nasi'a* (*riba* by way of deferment).[141] It can be agreed that the price will be paid within two or three days. Payment may even be postponed for longer than that, provided the delay is not a condition of the contract.[142] This is a peculiarity of Maliki teaching, for no other school of law seems to admit or even tolerate a postponed payment of a *salam* price.

Delivery of a *salam* object ought to be postponed for a length of time known to both parties. The majority of Malikis say that such delay should not be less than fifteen days,[143] whereas others speak of two or three days as a minimum.[144] If the debtor/vendor decides to discharge his obligation before the agreed term, the purchaser is entitled to refuse delivery.[145] Fixing a delivery place is not a requisite for the validity of *salam*.[146] When one of the contracting parties alleges that there is an agreement about a given place, his word is given credit. When neither of the parties alleges the existence of such an agreement, then the vendor's choice of a delivery place is retained. This is not unanimously accepted by Maliki authors. Sahnun qualified the first point by teaching that the vendor is to be believed if he alleges that the agreed place is the place where the contract was concluded and Abu 'l-Faraj dissented on the second point by teaching that if neither of the parties alleges that the place of delivery is the place where the contract was concluded then the two parties have to exchange oaths. If both parties take the oath, the contract is cancelled.[147] Pledge and guarantee are valid securities, as quoted in *al-Mughni*.[148]

Hanbali *salam*. For the Hanbalis it is not necessary that a *salam* object be in existence at the time the contract is concluded, provided it is habitually available at delivery time.[149] Any article which can be determined by description pursuant to the Hanbali criteria (i.e. determination of genus, species, condition, colour, country of origin and other features which can have effect on the price or the use) can be the subject-matter of *salam*. Thus not only weighable or measurable articles are acceptable subject-matter, but also articles accounted by number (even when not alike), fruit, foodstuffs,

[139] Ibid., p. 204.
[140] Ibn Juzay, *Qawanin*, p. 294.
[141] Ibid.
[142] Ibn Rushd, *Bidayat al-mujtahid*, Vol. II, p. 202.
[143] Jaziri, *al-Fiqh 'ala al-madhahib*, Vol. II, p. 313.
[144] Ibn Rushd, *Bidayat al-mujtahid*, Vol. II, p. 203.
[145] Ibid., p. 207. [146] Ibid., p. 204. [147] Ibid., p. 208.
[148] Ibn Qudama, *al-Mughni*, Vol. IV, p. 342.
[149] Ibid., p. 326.

animals and meat, but not jewellery or precious stones, as these cannot be accurately described.[150]

Payment in *salam* should be made at the meeting of the contracting parties.[151] For the majority of Hanbali authors, payment should be in currency and not personal chattels.[152] The subject-matter cannot also be currency, otherwise there is necessarily *riba al-nasi'a* (*riba* by way of deferment), for *salam* necessarily involves deferment in the exchange of the countervalues.[153] *Salam* is intended to be a deferred transaction[154] and the delay ought to be of the kind which has some impact on the price, such as one month.[155] It cannot be trivial, for example a delay of one day, except when the subject-matter is of the kind which is required daily, such as bread or meat.[156] If the debtor/vendor offers to discharge his obligation before the agreed time has elapsed, the purchaser is entitled to refuse delivery if he expects to suffer damage by accepting an early delivery, either because the subject-matter is fruit, food or animal which he would have to consume before the agreed time or because storing the subject-matter would cause expense. If, however, no good reason can be invoked, then the purchaser has to accept early delivery.[157]

Fixing a delivery place is not a requisite for the validity of *salam*. If such a place is not fixed, then the place where *salam* was concluded is chosen as the delivery place unless the parties agree on another place.[158] Hanbali authors are divided on the question of allowing pledge or guarantee as security for a *salam*; Ibn Qudama inclines towards permission.[159]

Ibadi *salam*. Weighable or measurable articles normally available to the public can be a *salam* object. Articles which are naturally perishable, such as seasonal articles, e.g. grapes or fresh figs, cannot be a *salam* object, for dealing with them introduces a strong element of *gharar*: it is not certain whether they will be in existence at delivery date. Some Ibadi authors qualify this opinion by teaching that dealing in seasonal articles can be lawful, provided the term coincides with the season when such articles reappear. Fresh fish and game meat are not valid *salam* objects, for their availability is in doubt at delivery date.[160] Dissimilar articles accounted by number cannot be the object of *salam*,[161] nor can animals.[162] As for chattels

150 Ibid., pp. 305ff.
151 Jaziri, *al-Fiqh 'ala al-madhahib*, Vol II, p. 305.
152 Ibn Qudama, *al-Mughni*, Vol. IV, p. 332.
153 Ibid., pp. 331–2. 154 Ibid., p. 321.
155 al-Bahuti, *al-Rawd al-murbi'*, Vol. II, p. 188.
156 Ibid.
157 Ibn Qudama, *al-Mughni*, Vol. IV, p. 339.
158 al-Bahuti, *al-Rawd al-murbi'*, Vol. II, p. 189.
159 Ibn Qudama, *al-Mughni*, Vol. IV, pp. 342–3.
160 al-Shammakhi, *al-Idah*, Vol. III, pp. 360–1.
161 Ibid., p. 361. 162 Ibid., p. 364.

(ʿ*urud*) other than those which are weighable or measurable, there is a controversy regarding their eligibility as a *salam* object.[163] One Ibadi author authorizes *salam* whose subject-matter is animals or chattels, provided that they can be determined accurately by description.[164]

Only currency can be a *salam* price[165] and payment should take place at the meeting of the parties.[166] The minimum required time for delivery in *salam* is three days[167] and the maximum is the period for which the subject-matter is most likely to last.[168] If the debtor/vendor offers to discharge his obligation before the agreed time has elapsed, Ibadi authors are divided between allowing the purchaser to accept an early delivery and forbidding it on the ground that it amounts to *riba*.[169]

It does not seem that the Ibadis require the determination of a delivery place as requisite for the validity of *salam*. When such a place is undetermined, al-Shammakhi is of the opinion that the purchaser's place of residence is a valid delivery place.[170] Before the time set for payment elapses, it is unlawful for the purchaser to receive a pledge as a security for *salam* but he can validly request a guarantee. However, a pledged object in the hand of the guarantor is lawful. The reason for the distinction is that a pledge in the former case is viewed by Ibadis as amounting to *riba*, whereas if the pledge is in the guarantor's hand the danger of *riba* is dispelled.[171]

Sale where subject-matter or price may be determined by viewing: *bayʿ juzaf*

A sale is *juzaf* when performed notwithstanding the fact that the sale object or the price, when in currency, is assessed by mere viewing and not through the normal means for such assessment, namely weight, measure or number. *Bayʿ juzaf* is often described as being the sale of an undetermined quantity. It is probably more accurate to say that it is a sale whereby one of the countervalues is roughly determined by mere viewing: classic examples of *bayʿ juzaf* are the sale of a heap of wheat inspected by the contracting parties but not measured, or the sale of something for a handful of uncounted currency.

Bayʿ juzaf should have been, in principle, totally unacceptable by Sharia standards; this is not so. It is tolerated by the various schools of law as a matter of necessity (*darura*), such as when it is practically impossible or

163 Ibid., pp. 361ff.
164 al-Basyani, *Mukhtasar*, p. 179.
165 al-Shammakhi, *al-Idah*, Vol. III, p. 357.
166 Ibid.; al-Basyani, *Mukhtasar*, p. 180.
167 al-Basyani, *Mukhtasar*, p. 180; al-Shammakhi, *al-Idah*, Vol. III, p. 366.
168 al-Shammakhi, *al-Idah*, Vol. III, p. 366.
169 al-Salimi, *Jawhar al-nizam*, Vol. II, pp. 336–7 (edn revised by Ibrahim Atfish).
170 al-Shammakhi, *al-Idah*, Vol. III, pp. 369–70.
171 Ibid., pp. 385–6.

extremely difficult to measure, weigh or count the object of the sale (for example, sale of pelts, hides, unharvested agricultural products, and so on). Other factors helped in making *bay' juzaf* lawful, such as the wish to close a deal promptly or even to add a flavour of acceptable risk to commercial ventures. Therefore it is not surprising that the various schools of law endeavoured to regulate this kind of sale and produced, as usual, some divergences.

Hanafis. For them, articles whose quantity is determined by way of weight, measure or number and which are called *muqadarat* can be sold *juzaf* (Article 220, *Majalla*), provided that neither the vendor nor the purchaser has knowledge of the exact quantity involved in the transaction. However, when the vendor alone is aware of the exact quantity of the sale object, the sale remains valid in the opinion of Abu Hanifa and Shafii,[172] but is viewed with aversion (*karahiyya*). Furthermore, when the sale object consists of articles which mainly belong to the category of *muqadarat*, the vendor may validly say to the purchaser, "I have sold to you a measure [or specified measures] of this heap of wheat", even though the heap is of undetermined quantity, provided such lack of determination does not cause a dispute.[173] The situation is different with regard to dissimilar articles, such as animals or garments. In such instances the subject-matter should be determined individually; it is not enough to say to the purchaser, "I have sold to you an animal from this herd or a garment from this shelf", for animals and garments are different from each other, and a *bay' juzaf* would most probably end in a dispute.[174]

When the price is currency, it may, in the Hanafi view, be exchanged *juzaf*, that is after mere viewing and with no counting.[175] The most probable reason for the Hanafi tolerance is the favourable attitude of this school towards the right of option (*haqq al-khiyar*). Here again the purchaser is granted the right to rescind the transaction if he is not satisfied after proper assessment of the sale object.[176]

Malikis. The rules of *bay' juzaf* are much more stringent under Maliki teaching. *Bay' juzaf* is allowed when its subject-matter is an article whose quantity can be determined by either measure or weight and furthermore is not sought for its individuality but is similar to others.[177] Thus articles accounted by number, such as animals, garments and currency cannot be sold *juzaf*[178] except when the sale object is trivial, such as the sale of a few

172 Mahmasani, *al-Awza'i*, p. 273.
173 al-Kasani, *Bada'i'*, Vol. v, p. 158.
174 Sanhuri, *Masadir al-haqq*, Vol. III, pp. 64–6.
175 Baz, *Sharh al-Majalla*, under Article 141.
176 Ibid., under Article 218.
177 Ibn Rushd, *Bidayat al-mujtahid*, Vol. II, p. 158.
178 Ibid., p. 159.

pomegranates or bananas.[179] Both the vendor and the purchaser should have, more or less, the same degree of knowledge of the subject-matter; if the vendor but not the purchaser knew the exact quantity involved in the transaction, the transaction would be invalid.[180] Finally, the purchaser has no option to rescind *bayʿ juzaf* except for defect or misrepresentation.[181]

Shafiis. For Shafiis, a heap of grain, flour or walnuts can be sold *juzaf* when neither the vendor nor the purchaser knows the exact quantity involved in the sale, provided that both have viewed the sale object. External viewing is sufficient, for all the parts are alike and furthermore it is difficult to inspect them all, contrary to the case of a garment – which can be easily spread out and inspected.[182] Nevertheless, if the vendor tells the purchaser, "I have sold to you some of this heap of grain", the sale is invalid owing to the *gharar* it imports; for it is not known whether this "some" is little or great.[183] If the vendor tells the purchaser, "I have sold to you this heap of grain or ten measures of this heap", that is valid, even though the exact quantum of the heap is unknown, for material *gharar* is dispelled by viewing.[184]

Apparently, Shafiis make a broad and general distinction between like and dissimilar articles. Thus one or more animals out of a herd cannot be sold *juzaf* for one animal differs from another. However, the entire herd can be sold *juzaf*.[185]

The purchaser enjoys the option of rescinding the sale only in the event that the subject-matter has suffered a defect or the purchaser himself was the victim of misrepresentation.[186] It will be recalled that the Hanafis, contrary to the Shafiis and other schools of law whose views are examined here, consider *bayʿ juzaf* as being non-binding (*ghayr lazim*), i.e. the purchaser can always change his mind and rescind the transaction after exact assessment of the quantity involved.

Like the Hanafis, the Shafiis practise *bayʿ juzaf* with currency as the consideration roughly determined by simple viewing.[187]

Hanbalis. Hanbali teaching on the matter of *bayʿ juzaf* does not differ much from the Shafii one. Sale of a heap of grain *juzaf* is allowed when the vendor and the purchaser are both unaware of the exact quantity involved; the reason is that they each attain the same degree of knowledge by viewing,[188] and there is no harm done by not viewing the heap's interior. Indeed, it would be obnoxious to ask for such viewing, since all grains of the heap are the same. The position is different when a garment is the subject-matter, for

179 al-Kashnawi, *Ashal al-madarik*, Vol. II, p. 241.
180 Ibn Rushd, *Bidayat al-mujtahid*, Vol. II, p. 159.
181 al-Kashnawi, *Ashal al-madarik*, Vol. II, p. 242.
182 al-Nawawi, *al-Majmuʿ*, Vol. IX, p. 312.
183 Ibid., p. 309. 184 Ibid., pp. 310–11. 185 Ibid., p. 313.
186 Ibid., p. 314. 187 Ibid., pp. 312 and 328.
188 Ibn Qudama, *al-Mughni*, Vol. IV, p. 137.

a garment can easily be spread out and inspected.[189] Articles and currencies alike can be sold *juzaf* when the required conditions are fulfilled.[190] The purchaser has the right to rescind the transaction when there is a defect[191] or when the purchaser was not aware that the vendor knew the exact quantity involved in the transaction. If the purchaser did know that the vendor was aware of the exact quantum, then he would lose his right of option.[192]

Ibadis. The Ibadi author al-Shammakhi reminds us that the sale of corporeal articles (*aʿyan*) is allowed only after knowledge of some aspect of the subject-matter. Nothing of what is measured or weighed or counted or planted in the ground can be sold except when the quantity involved in the transaction is known to the vendor and the purchaser. Knowledge of the quantity by guess, which is called *juzaf*, is acceptable with regard to some articles and unacceptable with regard to others. Articles which are measured or weighed can be the subject of *juzaf* when it is the quantity which is important, and not the individual units.[193] Articles sold by number seem to be excluded from *bayʿ juzaf*,[194] as are animals, dinars and dirhams. Articles which can in no way be assessed by way of measure, weight or number such as pelts, cords, and so on, as well as manufactured articles, ought to be sold *juzaf*.[195]

5 Keeping effective control over the exchanged countervalues

The subject-matter

Under Sharia law, that which the vendor is not in a position to hand over to the purchaser cannot be a sale object. This rule is unanimously adopted by the various schools of law, with a few limited exceptions which will be seen in the course of analysing the rule in more detail. The only way to do so is, as usual, to examine the various examples quoted by the authors who have discussed the matter. But once more it should be borne in mind that the reason why all quoted examples are drawn from the sale contract is that sale is the typical form of contract under Sharia law.

Examples most often quoted by Islamic jurisprudence are the following:

(a) The sale of an escaped slave or an escaped animal is invalid. This is the teaching of the Hanafis, Hanbalis,[196] Shafiis[197] and Ibadis.[198] Only Malik, as reported by

189 Ibid. 190 Ibid., p. 138.
191 Ibid., p. 139. 192 Ibid.
193 al-Shammakhi, *al-Idah*, Vol. III, pp. 120–1.
194 al-Basyani, *Mukhtasar*, p. 179.
195 al-Shammakhi, *al-Idah*, Vol. III, pp. 122–3.
196 Ibn Qudama, *al-Mughni*, Vol. IV, pp. 221–2.
197 al-Nawawi, *al-Majmuʿ*, Vol. IX, pp. 283–5.
198 al-Shammakhi, *al-Idah*, Vol. III, p. 70; al-Salimi, *Jawhar al-nizam*, Vol. II, p. 310 (edn revised by I. Atfish).

Ibn Rushd,[199] admitted the sale of an escaped animal or slave, provided the parties know of the approximate whereabouts of the sale object and provided, furthermore, that payment of the price is deferred until the escaped animal or slave is placed in the purchaser's possession.

(b) The sale of a bird in the air is also invalid, whether or not it is the vendor's property and whether or not it is accustomed to return to its nest; that is, according to Ibn Qudama, the teaching of all schools of law.[200] Ibn Qudama[201] was keen to distinguish between the sale object which cannot be handed over to the purchaser because it is out of sight in a remote place and the sale object, such as a bird in the air, which cannot be handed over because of lack of control over it. In the first instance, the sale object can always be brought forth if time and expenses are not spared, whereas in the latter situation the subject-matter of the sale is its own master and cannot be controlled.

(c) The sale of fish in water is disallowed by the Hanbalis, Hanafis, Malikis,[202] Shafiis[203] and Ibadis.[204]. This kind of sale *can* be validly performed if (1) the fish is owned by the vendor; (2) the water is shallow so the fish can be seen and appraised; and finally (3) the fish can be easily caught.[205]

(d) The sale of the young of an animal still unborn when the mother is not part of the sale and also the sale of milk still in the udders is disallowed for two reasons: the first is want of knowledge with regard to the characteristics of the sale object and the second reason is the fact that the subject-matter cannot be delivered at will to the purchaser.[206] Nevertheless, Malik appeared to allow the sale of milk still in the udders provided that it is for a specified number of days, involves more than one animal and provided, furthermore, that the average amount of milk produced per day by the animals involved is known.[207]

(e) The sale of a stallion's sperm is disallowed by Hanbalis, Hanafis and Shafiis although it seems tolerated by the Malikis.[208]

The price

In the same way as they should have control over the subject-matter, the contracting parties should also have an effective control over the price. This requirement is particularly relevant when the purchaser in a sale contract or, indeed, the party who did not deliver his promised payment forthwith in all sorts of bilateral transactions, invites the vendor to receive satisfaction from a third party. In that way the obligation to pay the price shifts from the purchaser to an outsider. When this substitution occurs, the question is to

199 Ibn Rushd, *Bidayat al-mujtahid*, Vol. II, p. 158.
200 Ibn Qudama, *al-Mughni*, Vol. IV, p. 222; al-Nawawi, *al-Majmu'*, Vol. IX, p. 283.
201 Ibn Qudama, *al-Mughni*, Vol. IV, pp. 222–3.
202 Ibid., p. 223.
203 al-Nawawi, *al-Majmu'*, Vol. IX, p. 283.
204 al-Shammakhi, *al-Idah*, Vol. III, p. 69; al-Basyani, *Mukhtasar*, p. 178.
205 Ibn Qudama, *al-Mughni*, Vol. IV, p. 223.
206 Ibid., p. 230; Ibn Juzay, *Qawanin*, p. 282; al-Sarakhsi, *al-Mabsut*, Vol. XII, p. 194; al-Shammakhi, *al-Idah*, Vol. III, p. 70; al-Basyani, *Mukhtasar*, p. 178.
207 Ibn Rushd, *Bidayat al-mujtahid*, Vol. II, p. 158.
208 Ibn Qudama, *al-Mughni*, Vol. IV, pp. 232–3.

know how much the contracting parties have power and control over the new debtor, who was not part of their initial transaction, and ultimately how far payment of such a price is secured. The operation of substituting for the person of a debtor the person of another is known in Islamic law as *hawalat al-dayn* or assignment of debt. Possibly the word *aval* takes its origin from the Arabic word *hawala*.

Hawalat al-dayn was studied and regulated by various scholars attached to different schools of law.[209] The definition given by the *Majalla* to *hawalat al-dayn* is that it amounts to the transfer of a debt from one *dhimma* to another *dhimma* (Article 673). In Islamic law *dhimma* has two related meanings. From a subjective angle, it is the qualification to bear obligations and enjoy rights recognized in each human being at birth; it is also, from an objective angle, the recipient of obligations *dayn* (incorporeal properties), as opposed to obligations *ʿayn*, which correspond more or less to things real, determined in their individuality, such as a piece of land, animals and the like. Because *hawalat al-dayn* is the transfer of a debt from one *dhimma* to another *dhimma*, such a debt cannot be other than an incorporeal property (*dayn*) such as a specific amount of money or quantity of grain not actually present at the meeting of the parties or if present not actually isolated from other amounts or quantities (Article 158, *Majalla*). It cannot be property *ʿayn*, which is normally transferred by the handing over of the tangible property.[210] This tangible property is not an obligation stored in the *dhimma* but a corpus individually defined. Assignment of a debt (*hawalat al-dayn*) imports transfer of the right and the debt itself, according to the teaching of all but a few scholars.[211] The assigned debt should be defined, fixed, due and equal in quantity and quality to the debt which was the cause of the assignment.[212] Although it is, generally speaking, of normal occurrence for the third party who becomes the new debtor, by virtue of the assignment, to be a pre-existing debtor of the assignor, this is not a requisite for most schools of law except the Shafii one.[213]

Suftaja (bill of exchange) is the most common instance where the new

[209] Although the assignment of right (*hawalat dayn al-daʾin*) is not of direct interest to our topic it is worthy of notice that Islamic law, except for the Maliki and Ibadi (al-Shammakhi, *al-Idah*, Vol. III, pp. 422ff.) schools of law, does not allow the assignment of right except in specific circumstances, which are numerous according to the Hanafi teaching and very few according to the Shafii one (Mahmasani, *The General Theory*, pp. 595–9); whereas the Hanbali school of law does not allow the assignment of right to other than the debtor himself, whether with or without consideration (Ibn Qudama, *al-Mughni*, Vol. V, p. 659).

[210] Mahmasani, *The General Theory*, pp. 605–6.

[211] Ibid., pp. 606–7.

[212] Ibid., p. 606; al-Shammakhi, *al-Idah*, Vol. III, p. 398; Ibn Qudama, *al-Mughni*, Vol. IV, p. 577; al-Basyani, *Mukhtasar*, p. 179.

[213] *Sharh al-Majalla* by Ali Haydar under Article 686. For the Hanbalis when the new debtor is not a pre-existing debtor to the assignor, *hawala* amounts to a power of attorney with the authority to conclude a loan (al-Bahuti, *Kashshaf al-qinaʿ*, Vol. III, p. 385; Ibn Qudama, *al-Mughni*, Vol. IV, p. 579).

debtor is *not* a pre-existing assignor's debtor. *Suftaja* is defined as a loan of money repayable by the borrower to a person other than the lender (here lies its similarity to *hawala*) in a place different from the place where the money was handed over to the borrower. *Suftaja*'s main purpose is to avoid the risk of transporting the money and that purpose is reached by creating, besides the borrower's obligation to repay the money, another obligation, which is to pay that money to a person other than the lender. Because the lender derives from the *suftaja*, which is basically, as we must remember, a loan of money, such an extra advantage, it was regarded with some suspicion by the various schools of law, but not to the point of forbidding it.[214]

To what extent the discharge of the *dayn* object of the *hawala* (normally a sum of money in the *dhimma* but it could be any lawful incorporeal property) can be guaranteed is contingent upon the type of performed *hawala*, for not all assignments of debt are concluded in the same way or by agreement of all concerned parties. The different methods of concluding *hawalat al-dayn* will now be briefly examined.

***Hawala* by agreement of all concerned parties.** By "concerned parties" is meant the debtor-assignor (*muhil*), the creditor-assignee (*muhal lahu*) and the new debtor (*muhal ʿalaihi*). This is in principle the ideal situation, where all concerned parties consent to the substitution of a new debtor for the original one.

***Hawala* by agreement of the creditor and the new debtor.** The original debtor does not participate in this sort of *hawala*, which is not of common occurrence but can still be encountered. The prevailing opinion of the Hanafi school is that the agreement of the original debtor is unnecesary for the validity of the *hawala*.[215] The Ibadis hold the same view.[216] This opinion is not shared by the majority of schools of law, which on the contrary require the original debtor's agreement for the validity of this type of *hawala*.[217]

***Hawala* by agreement of the debtor-assignor (*muhil*) and the creditor-assignee (*muhal lahu*).** For the Hanafis this sort of *hawala* is contingent upon the new debtor's agreement, otherwise it is null and void (Article 682, *Majalla*). For the Malikis,[218] Shafiis,[219] Hanbalis[220] and Ibadis[221] *hawala* concluded without the new debtor's prior agreement is lawful.

214 See Chapter 2, Section 2, n. 53.
215 Mahmasani, *The General Theory*, p. 603.
216 al-Shammakhi, *al-Idah*, Vol. III, p. 424.
217 al-Hattab, *Mawahib al-jalil*, Vol. V, p. 90; Ibn Qudama, *al-Mughni*, Vol. IV, p. 576; al-Rafiʿi, *Fath al-ʿaziz* in margin of al-Nawawi's *Majmuʿ*, Vol. X, p. 338.
218 Ibn Rushd, *Bidayat al-mujtahid*, Vol. II, p. 248.
219 al-Rafiʿi, *Fath al-ʿaziz* in al-Nawawi, *Majmuʿ*, Vol. X, p. 339.
220 Ibn Qudama, *al-Mughni*, Vol. IV, p. 583.
221 al-Shammakhi, *al-Idah*, Vol. III, p. 426.

***Hawala* by agreement of the debtor-assignor (*muhil*) and the new debtor (*muhal ʿalaihi*).** This *hawala* is contingent upon the creditor's agreement, according to the teachings of Abu Hanifa, Malikis and Shafiis[222] and according to the teaching of the Ibadi school.[223] Ibn Hanbal holds a different view, which can be summed up as follows: when the new debtor is solvent, it is not requisite to obtain the creditor's agreement to the *hawala*.[224]

Normally the effect of *hawalat al-dayn* is to discharge the debtor-assignor (*muhil*) from the debts he owes to the creditor-assignee (*muhal lahu*). *Hawala* can also occur with the condition that the debtor-assignor (*muhil*) shall remain liable for the debt, in which circumstance *hawala* is assimilated to a guarantee and the creditor-assignee has the right to claim settlement from either the debtor-assignor or the new debtor.[225] When the liability of the debtor-assignor is not retained, his discharge from the debt has the consequence of releasing the guarantors, if any, pursuant to Article 690 of the *Majalla*.

For Ibn Hanbal and al-Shafiʿi, when the new debtor is solvent the creditor-assignee has no recourse whatsoever against the debtor-assignor in the event that the debt is not settled by this new debtor. Discharge of the debtor-assignor is total and irrevocable unless his guarantee was obtained specifically for the case of non-payment.[226] This is in principle the Maliki opinion, with the difference that for Malik the creditor-assignee has the right of recourse against the debtor-assignor in the case of misrepresentation and of assignment to a new debtor who was already bankrupt before the *hawala* was concluded.[227]

For the Hanafis, *hawala* in principle discharges the debtor-assignor, with the exception that the creditor-assignee has a right of recourse against him in the event that his claim is in danger of failing either for the reason that the new debtor is insolvent or because he denies the existence of the *hawala* and no proof of its existence is in the creditor's hand, or because the new debtor has died bankrupt, or even, according to Abu Hanifa's two companions, because he became bankrupt while alive.[228]

Finally *hawala*, according to Ibadis, discharges the debtor-assignor once and for all provided the creditor-assignee has accepted the *hawala*.[229] If the new debtor is not a pre-existing debtor of the assignor, he cannot ask the latter to pay him the amount of *hawala* before he has himself paid it to the

222 Mahmasani, *The General Theory*, p. 604.
223 al-Shammakhi, *al-Idah*, Vol. III, pp. 422–3 (note).
224 Ibn Qudama, *al-Mughni*, Vol. IV, pp. 582–3.
225 Ibn Qudama, *al-Mughni*, Vol. IV, p. 582.
226 Ibn Qayyim al-Jawziyya, *Iʿlam al-muwaqqiʿin*, Vol. IV, p. 32; al-Rafiʿi, *Fath al-ʿaziz*, in al-Nawawi, *Majmuʿ*, Vol. X, p. 344; al-Shafiʿi, *al-Umm*, Vol. III, p. 203.
227 al-Hattab, *Mawahib al-jalil*, Vol. V, p. 95.
228 Mahmasani, *The General Theory*, pp. 608–9.
229 al-Basyani, *Mukhtasar*, p. 312; al-Shammakhi, *al-Idah*, Vol. III, p. 427.

assignee. Reimbursement should always take place in the same genus as the money of payment, e.g. when silver is assigned but payment was carried out in gold, reimbursement of the new debtor by the assignor should be in silver (Article 698, *Majalla*).[230]

230 al-Bahuti, *Kashshaf al-qina'*, Vol. III, p. 385; al-Shammakhi, *al-Idah*, Vol. III, p. 442.

APPENDIX 2

Sources of the prohibition of *gharar*

The Quran (s. II:219 and s. V:93) prohibited games of hazard (*maysir*, which literally means "getting something too easily", "getting a profit without working for it"); and the Prophet, according to widely postulated traditions, forbade the sale of an escaped slave or animal, the sale of a bird in the air or a fish in the water, the sale of what the vendor is not in a position to deliver, *bayʿ al-hasah*, *bayʿ munabadha*, *bayʿ mulamasa*,[1] *bayʿ muhaqala*,[2] *bayʿ mukhadara*,[3] the sale of the young still unborn when the mother is not part of the sale, the sale of milk in the udders and the sale of the stallion's sperm.

The rationale behind the prohibition of all these sales is the fear of *gharar* (uncertainty; risk; speculation), whether in the ability of the vendor to deliver the object of the sale as in the case of the stray animal or in the existence of the subject-matter as in the case of milk still in the udders or agricultural products which have not yet come to fruition, or in the characteristics, such as the sale of the stones of the dates without the fruit, or in the date of performance such as the sale of the young yet to be born.

At a later stage, the process of reasoning was over-simplified and the non-existence (*ʿadam*) of the subject-matter was (improperly) considered as a sufficient cause for nullifying the transaction, with no regard to the element of risk (*gharar*). Because the subject-matter was non-existent when the transaction was concluded it was assumed that there was no need to research whether or not its inception was doubtful.

1 For the meaning of *bayʿ al-hasah*, *bayʿ munabadha* and *bayʿ mulamasa*, see p. 51 above.

2 *Bayʿ muhaqala* is the sale of agricultural products against an amount of seeds of the same species.

3 *Bayʿ mukhadara* is the sale of non-mature agricultural products and the sale of dates which have not shown signs of readiness, when not accompanied by the requisite that they should be picked up with no delay.

CHAPTER 4

A financial system based on Islamic ethics

1 A short survey

The prohibition of *riba* and *gharar*, once it came into conflict with business as practised, must have greatly embarrassed devout Muslims, as it continues to embarrass them today. The temptation to disregard Islamic teaching in this respect was, and still is, enticing: for the financial system which prevails up to now, at least within a capitalist society, relies heavily on "interest", which is the modern epitome of *riba*, while speculative transactions are still attractive for the large return they may provide. In addition to the lure of greater profit, the insurance contract, which is a typical form of speculative transaction, is much needed in contemporary business.

It is erroneous, and even the apologists do not allege the contrary, to imagine that immediately following the ban on *riba* and *gharar* people gave up pricing the loan of idle capital or dealing with aleatory contracts. A clear indication of the limited effect that the religious ban had in practice is to be found in the infinite variety of legal devices (*hiyal*) invented by scholars in order to circumvent the ban. However, it is only fair to say that not all orthodox schools of law accept the validity of such devices: only the Hanafi and Shafii schools do so. Nevertheless, most non-Muslims writing on Islamic law saw only this negative aspect of the matter and were prompt to tax Muslims with shallowness and religious hypocrisy. Such critics failed to see other aspects, which, if they had been perceived would necessarily have mitigated their criticism and prompted them to abandon anecdotal accounts in favour of an overall view of the problem. What the critics failed to see was that the ban on *riba* and *gharar* amounted to the condemnation of an entire financial and economic system which for various reasons survived despite the ban. Such condemnation was not, however, followed by positive steps proposing a lawful comprehensive system as a substitute for the prevailing one. Capitalism cannot be Islamized simply by abolishing interest and aleatory transactions; new proposals were needed, but unfortunately were not forthcoming. The other aspect which escaped the critics was that all over the world a significant number of Muslims refused to deal with *riba* and *gharar*, despite the lack of an alternative option that could provide them with an opportunity for a corresponding return. Even today many Muslims who have their savings deposited in banks which pay and charge interest relinquish the right of taking their earned interest, for it is forbidden (*haram*). However, it is unfair and unrealistic to expect Muslims to refrain collectively and permanently from being involved in *riba* and *gharar* as long as the basic foundation of the ruling economic order continues to be interest and speculation. In order that the ban on *riba* and *gharar* should be effective, observance of it should be a normal occurrence and not something requiring a permanent effort of self-denial. It was thought that this would result from the elaboration of a new scheme which leaves no practical function to *riba* and *gharar*. The necessary first step towards this elaboration was considered by Muslim economists to be the re-organization of the banking system on the basis of Islamic ethics.

The earliest references to such re-organization were made during the 1940s.[1] The first Islamic bank in modern times in the Arab world was established in Egypt in the Delta town of Mit Ghamr in 1963, but was wound up a few years later for political reasons. The Egyptian experience was resumed in the early 1970s in a different field by the setting up of the Nasser Social Bank, which is initially, as noted by R. Cooper,[2] a social welfare organization rather than a commercial venture, for its basic objective is a *qard hasan* (i.e. an interest-free loan granted to the poor when faced with exceptional expenses arising from illness, weddings or funerals). The oldest commercial interest-free bank still in operation, the Dubai Islamic Bank, was founded some ten years ago. It was followed within a short time by a string of Islamic banks operating in both the East and the West. A Committee appointed by the central banks of Islamic countries has drafted a model Islamic Companies Code[3] which all interest-free banks are urged to adopt. Pakistan was the first state to initiate the Islamization of its economic and banking systems, in 1979,[4] followed by the Sudan in 1982.

Practically speaking, what Islamic banks are allowed or forbidden to do is known in broad, general terms: they cannot pay interest on the funds they receive, or lend their money for interest, or invest in bonds, debentures or through any other form of investment involving either *riba* or *gharar*. Moreover they are not allowed to participate in investments made by persons who give or receive interest or to be involved in any operation which introduces a material element of *gharar*. The new function that interest-free banks have to assume is to share with the depositors the risk of their common

1 M. N. Siddiqi, *Muslim Economic Thinking*, pp. 29–30.

2 *Euromoney*, December Issue, 1982, p. 123.

3 Ibnul Hasan, "A bold private initiative", in *Dar al Maal al Islami and Islamic Economic and Financial Institutions*, p. 24.

4 Nawazish ʿAli Zaidi, "Islamic Banking – Challenge and Opportunity", in *Dar al Maal*, p. 43.

investment and split the resulting profits or bear part of the losses, instead of assuming the bank's traditional function as simple intermediary between savers and investors. An interest-free bank which is the recipient of current accounts and savings deposits (i.e. those not intended for investment) guarantees that the assets shall be redelivered undamaged to the depositors. As for investment deposits, the bank is not liable to the account holders for the principal of such accounts (nor indeed for the expected return), except in case of negligence or wilful and conscious wrongdoing or breach of the agreed account conditions.

It is therefore apparent that the existing world banking system and the fiscal legislation in effect in Western countries are not compatible with the objectives and characteristics of interest-free banks. However, an interesting test case is now being experienced in Denmark, where the Islamic Bank International was authorized in 1983 to operate a banking activity based on Islamic Sharia, but within the existing Danish legislation, with no special concessions or exceptions granted. Whether the Danish test is a success or a failure, it remains a fact that mere toleration by an alien system is certainly not the Islamic Banks' ultimate objective. What these banks aim at is finding a satisfactory operational technique which will be lenient enough to infiltrate the established system and powerful enough to be taken into proper consideration. Will they succeed in their quest? The answer will probably be known soon enough, for their costly venture cannot last long if it does not prosper.

What is now available is a comprehensive technique, still in the process of being adjusted, which is put into practice by interest-free banks in the Islamic and Third World countries where room was secured for them by way of exceptions and special authorization granted by the local banking or financing authorities. Pursuant to this technique, some conventional banking operations, such as keeping teller's cash, taking non-interest-bearing demand deposits, cashing cheques, providing safe keeping, transfers, letters of credit (all of which are performed for service charges when not free), would continue to be remunerated in that way within the Islamic banking system, as interest is not involved. (The service charge should in no way be related to the financial value of the service, such as for example by being made proportional to the sum involved, for this would amount to *riba*; however, the service charge could be in proportion to the magnitude of the service as actually rendered.) Other banking operations need to be adjusted to Islamic standards. An example is the procedure for bills of exchange, for which one of the proposed solutions was to advance cash to the drawer of the bill of exchange on the basis of *mudaraba* (commenda partnership) claiming for the bank a modest share of the profits expected from the transaction;[5] another proposed solution is to have these services provided by nationalized

[5] M. N. Siddiqi, *Issues in Islamic Banking*, pp. 28–9.

banks which will charge only their expenses. Funds of an interest-free bank will be employed either in investments undertaken under the banks' direct control or in participation-financing.

The new technique comprises a category of operations peculiar to Islamic *fiqh*; they consist of: *musharaka* (partnership), *murabaha* (cost-plus-profit contract), *ijara* (lease contract), *ijara wa-iqtina'* (hire purchase contract), *qard hasan* (interest-free loan), *takaful* (mutual guarantee) and *mudaraba* (commenda partnership). All these concepts except the last one will be briefly reviewed; *mudaraba* will be examined in more detail. It is singled out for the reason that it represents an unchallenged Sharia concept besides being of great originality inside the interest-free economic system. Originality does not mean novelty, for *mudaraba* existed before the Prophet's time and flourished long after him. But the ingenuity lies in incorporating the *mudaraba* concept in the interest-free system so that it has become the main technique according to which mobilized funds from the public are rewarded and funds advanced by the bank to entrepreneurs taxed without running counter to Islamic ethics. It will have been seen by now that, pursuant to Sharia ethics, capital alone may not lawfully provide money (or indeed any other increase or advantage), whereas capital combined with the risk inherent in an enterprise may lawfully be productive provided that such an enterprise does not deal with banned subject-matters such as wine or pork meat, and provided furthermore that no material element of *gharar* accompanies the inception of the transaction which is used as the instrument of the projected enterprise. The concept of *mudaraba* has become the main vehicle for this combination of capital and enterprise and as such deserves to be looked at closely (see Section 3 below).

On the other hand, not all Islamic banks advocate *mudaraba* as a basic structure for their commercial operations; some banks take another view and consider *murabaha* to be more appropriate and less risky. The problem is that *murabaha* with deferred payment is regarded with aversion (*karahiyya*) by some Muslim authors when the price asked is higher than it would be with immediate cash payment, for the reason that pricing of time is in their view akin to *riba* (see pp. 94–5 below). The answer of those who favour *murabaha* with deferred payment is that no *riba* is involved, for in a *murabaha* transaction a commodity is sold for money and not money exchanged for money. They add furthermore that there is also an element of business risk which is involved in *murabaha* and which makes that concept even more distant from *riba*. This business risk is identified with the fact that the purchaser in a *murabaha* transaction is not compelled, according to these authors, to buy the commodity he has ordered but can always change his mind when the time comes for taking possession of the ordered commodity even though it satisfies all the requirements and standards he has asked for. (See pp. 67ff. above on the different views of the various schools of law with respect to the right of inspecting the object of the sale when it is not visible at the meeting of the contracting parties but is made available at a later stage.)

The Islamic financial institutions

The present banking system in practice in most Western and Eastern countries does not allow commercial banks to engage in any speculative transaction or in commercial and industrial operations other than purely monetary ones; therefore some of the aforementioned Islamic concepts cannot be utilized by interest-free banks operating within the existing banking system. Moreover, it is extremely cumbersome, if not impracticable, from an orthodox accounting perspective to isolate from the bulk of the operations of a given bank a single transaction whose profits are meant to be shared between the bank and the client involved in such transaction. All these limitations explain why one of the largest Islamic financial institutions, The Dar al Maal al Islami (D.M.I.), has resorted to an elaborate *modus operandi* which was described during numerous lectures delivered by the promoters and executives of Dar al Maal al Islami and in various brochures prepared by that institution. Thus D.M.I.'s scheme became better known, at least in theory, and can be summed up as follows. D.M.I. is a trust incorporated in the Bahamas in July 1981. Its business affairs are administered by D.M.I.S.A. (Switzerland), and its purpose is to conduct a general financial and trading business in conformity with Islam through the organization or acquisition and operation of Islamic investment companies, Islamic solidarity companies, Islamic banks, and other subsidiaries subsumed under the overall title of Islamic financial institutions. Financing is available to the clients of Islamic financial institutions through the operations outlined earlier (see p. 89 above). Islamic financial institutions can also be active in the international commodity exchanges, the international money markets and international leasing and trading opportunities, provided that the guidelines imposed by Islam are followed. (However, not all Muslim scholars approve of transactions with respect to commodity exchanges and international money markets owing to the elements of *riba* and material *gharar* which they consider to be involved.) Funds are mobilized by Islamic financial institutions through the following means.

(1) **The Islamic investment companies.** These offer to the public a participation in defined commenda partnerships (*mudaraba*) identified by the D.M.I. as "Trusts financing", where the public provides the funds while the investment companies supply the expertise and know-how. The public acquires participation certificates (*sukuk*) and net profits are split in what has become a customary usage: one-tenth to the Investment Company and nine-tenths to the holders of the participation certificates.

(2) **The Islamic solidarity companies.** These are an alternative to modern insurance and they function commercially on the same basis as *mudaraba*, with the particular aim of mobilizing the combined holdings of the participants in a given pool, in order to compensate one of them for the financial consequences of a risk if and when it materializes.

(3) **The Islamic banks** mobilize funds from the public through current and Islamic participating accounts. The current account pays no dividend; the Islamic participating account is either payable at a specified period after call, with various alternatives offered, or payable after a specified fixed period with alternatives also offered. The assets underlying participating accounts will be invested according to the principles of Sharia law, mostly in *mudaraba* ventures and the profits or losses shared between the bank and the participants according to a pre-agreed ratio.

Other major Islamic institutions, such as Kuwait Finance House, al-Baraka Group and al-Rajii Group operate in more or less the same manner, although sometimes using a different terminology, and sometimes with a greater reliance placed on *murabaha* rather than *mudaraba*.

2 The operations traditional to *fiqh* revived by Islamic financial institutions

Musharaka or *sharika*

Musharaka or *sharika* is normally translated into English as "partnership". However, Islamic financial institutions translate it as "Participation financing", in order to put more emphasis on one particular aspect of *musharaka* that will come to our attention later. Sharia divides partnership into two broad categories:

(a) Property partnership (*sharikat mulk*), which amounts, broadly speaking, to the joint ownership of a property without its joint exploitation, such as the joint ownership of a house transmitted, by devolution, to the heirs of a deceased person.
(b) Contractual partnership (*sharikat ʿaqd*), where emphasis is on the joint exploitation of capital and the joint participation in profits and losses and where joint ownership is a consequence of, and not a prerequisite for, the formation of the partnership.

It is the contractual partnership (*sharikat ʿaqd*) which is of interest to the present topic. When scholars study this sort of partnership they frequently differentiate such partnerships according to the object of the investment;[6] so that contractual partnerships are normally divided into:

6 Islamic jurisprudence (*fiqh*) makes no distinction between commercial and non-commercial partnerships – the rules and principles it has established apply to both categories.

(a) Finance partnership (*sharikat mal*), where the money is the main investment;
(b) labour partnership (*sharikat a'mal*) where the partnership investment consists fully or mainly of the work and skills of the partners; and
(c) credit partnership (*sharikat wujuh*) where credit alone is used for partnership investment.

Each of these – finance partnership, labour partnership and credit partnership – can take the form of an unlimited, unrestricted and equal partnership (the *mufawada* as understood by the Hanafis), or the form of a limited investment partnership (*'inan*).

A third form of partnership (in addition to property and contractual partnerships), i.e. *mudaraba* (commenda), is examined separately in the books of Islamic jurisprudence. This practice will be followed here also (see Section 3 of this chapter).

The *mufawada*, according to the Hanafis, is a partnership in which the partners enjoy complete equality, *inter alia*, in the areas of capital, management and right of disposition. Each *mufawada* partner is both the agent of and the guarantor for his colleague. The Maliki concept of *mufawada* is nearly the same as that of the Hanafis.[7] The Shafiis, however, consider *mufawada* partnership null and void,[8] mainly because the equality it advocates cannot be implemented in practice. The Hanbalis have conflicting views regarding *mufawada*. Ibn Qudama[9] maintained that the only lawful *mufawada* formula is one in which partners associate in all the different types of partnership investments or, in other words, when partners decide to combine money, labour and credit; each of these types being legal, it is perfectly legitimate to combine them all. Other Hanbali authors such as al-Futuhi[10] regard *mufawada* in the same light as the Hanafis, and a few other Hanbali scholars share the Shafii view in condemning that form of partnership. For the Ibadis *mufawada* consists of the unlimited association of two or more persons in all fields, each partner having equal authority over the properties of the other partner(s) and all profits and gains being divided among the partners except for inheritance, blood money (*diyya*) and dowry (*mahr*). Contrary to the Hanafi *mufawada*, some Ibadi authors do not believe that equality of capital and equality of shares in the profits are necessary.[11]

The *'inan* partnership is a contractual partnership whereby two or more partners contribute to a capital fund, either in money or in kind or in labour or in combining all or some of these investments. Teachings of the different

[7] Ibn Rushd, *Bidayat al-mujtahid*, Vol. II, pp. 254–5.
[8] al-Shafi'i, *al-Umm*, Vol. VII, p. 134.
[9] *al-Mughni*, Vol. V, pp. 29–30.
[10] *Muntaha al-iradat*, Vol. I, p. 470.
[11] al-Shammakhi, *al-Idah*, Vol. IV, pp. 40ff.

schools of law vary in this respect. For the Hanafis,[12] Malikis[13] and Hanbalis[14] a contribution to a *ʿinan*'s capital can take any of these forms of investment; it cannot be credit for the Malikis and Shafiis[15] and it cannot be chattels (*ʿurud*) for the Shafiis[16] nor labour.[17] Contribution to an Ibadi *ʿinan* could be envisaged other than in money terms provided that such contribution could be weighed and measured and provided that all contributions were of the same kind and value.[18] Partners in a *ʿinan* share the profits in the agreed manner and bear losses in proportion to their mutual contributions. Each partner is only the agent of and not a guarantor for his colleague(s) and this mutual agency is valid only in the area of business covered by the partnership or to the extent of their joint capital.

The agency that results from *ʿinan* is restricted to the partners' relationship, in the sense that only the partner who has concluded a transaction can sue the party with whom he has contracted, and the latter has no action except against the contracting partner.[19] This is because a *ʿinan* partnership implies mutual agency but not mutual surety. As a consequence, an individual partner does not become liable for that which is owed by his colleagues. Debts owed to and by each individual partner cannot be collected from or claimed by his associates. (The situation is different in a *mufawada* partnership, where each *mufawada* partner is both the agent of and the guarantor for his colleague(s), with the consequence that each partner is fully liable for the actions and commitments of the other(s) in all matters involved in the *mufawada*. The claims of third parties are thus actionable against any partner; and, conversely, any partner can press a claim against a third party, regardless of whether or not he was actually involved in the transaction which gave rise to that claim.)

There is an important exception to the fundamental principle governing *ʿinan* partnership; this principle, as already seen, dictates that a partner conducting a given transaction with a third party shall, in his relationship with the third party, bear the onus of and receive the benefit of such a transaction, and a partner who was not involved cannot interfere except as regards his relationship with the contracting partner. The exception is found in that form of *ʿinan* partnership where the partners' investment is their labour and which is called in Arabic *ʿinan sharikat aʿmal* (or *abdan*). For the Hanafis,[20] Malikis and Hanbalis[21] a *ʿinan sharikat aʿmal* is considered as a

[12] Jaziri, *al-Fiqh ʿala al-madhahib*, Vol. III, p. 68.
[13] Ibn Rushd, *Bidayat al-mujtahid*, Vol. II, pp. 252–5.
[14] N. Saleh, *The General Principles*, pp. 47–8.
[15] Ibn Rushd, *Bidayat al-mujtahid*, Vol. II, p. 255.
[16] Ibid., p. 252.
[17] Jaziri, *al-Fiqh ʿala al-madhahib*, Vol. III, p. 76.
[18] al-Shammakhi, *al-Idah*, Vol. IV, p. 34.
[19] Chafik Chéhata, *Théorie générale de l'obligation en droit musulman Hanéfite*, p. 281.
[20] Articles 1387 and 1388 of the *Majalla*.
[21] Ibn Qudama, *al-Mughni*, Vol. V, pp. 6–7.

mufawada partnership with regard to the work undertaken by one of the partners and the salary owed by the employer. The practical meaning of this is that when one of the partners undertakes to perform a work for an employer, the other partner is also bound by his undertaking. Furthermore, each of the partners is entitled to claim the total salary due for the work done, and if the employer pays the total salary to any one of the partners he is released from his obligation. This limited mutation of a *ʿinan sharikat aʿmal* into *mufawada* partnership does not apply to the Shafii *ʿinan*, which cannot validly exist with an investment consisting solely of labour and can hardly be attributed to the Ibadis, who are reluctant to acknowledge the validity of an investment consisting solely of labour;[22] in addition, they have an original view on *mufawada*.

The *musharaka* of the Islamic financial institutions is obviously the *ʿinan sharikat mal* or "finance-limited investment partnership" or, to use the terminology of the said Institutions, a "participation financing" where money is the main investment. In accordance with the terms of a "participation financing", the Islamic bank or institution will fund the equity capital, cash flow requirements, or both, for an agreed enterprise proposed by an entrepreneur client to the institution or bank. Profits will be shared between the two parties in the agreed ratio, and losses, if any, will be in proportion to the partners' shares in the partnership capital, as generally taught.[23]

Finally, it is worth noting that from the point of view of Islamic law no security can be taken from the partner as such; only one sort of security is allowed, and indeed required, by some Islamic banks, such as the Faisal Islamic Bank of Sudan, and that is a security against the risk of negligence or wilful wrongdoing of the partner or his non-compliance with the terms of the partnership contract. The business risk inherent in the partnership and its outcome cannot be secured.

Murabaha

Murabaha is generally defined as the sale of a commodity for the price at which the vendor has purchased it, with the addition of a stated profit known to both the vendor and the purchaser. It is a cost-plus-profit contract. Islamic financial institutions aim to make use of *murabaha* in circumstances where they will purchase raw materials, goods or equipment etc. and sell them to a client at cost, plus a negotiated profit margin[24] to be paid normally by instalments. With *murabaha*, Islamic financial institutions are no longer to

22 al-Shammakhi, *al-Idah*, Vol. IV, pp. 49–51.

23 For a detailed account of the distribution of profits and losses see N. Saleh, *General Principles*, pp. 62–5.

24 Prince Muhammad al-Faysal al-Saʿud in his speech delivered to the Conference of the Arab Bankers Association in London, 7 and 8 June 1982.

share profits or losses, but instead assume the capacity of a classic financial intermediary.[25]

The legality of *murabaha* is not questioned by any of the schools of law mentioned in the present book. There are of course differences in the details, some of which will come to our attention. However, the use of *murabaha* as a credit vehicle by the Islamic financial institutions has been regarded with apprehension by some Muslim authors, for example M. Siddiqi, who contended that the simple fact that *murabaha* enables a buyer to finance his purchase with deferred payment, as against accepting a mark-up on the market price of the commodity, means that the financier, in this case the Islamic bank, earns a predetermined profit without bearing any risk.[26] That is a good example of the sometimes thin line which separates legitimate trade from illegal *riba*. The only factor which, in the opinion of the conservative jurists, would probably transform *murabaha* into a legal device (*hila*) used to circumvent the prohibition of taking interest is pricing the time factor. That occurs when, in addition to the initial price of the commodity and other recognized expenses and legitimate profit, an increase is accounted in order to compensate for the delayed payment of the *murabaha* purchase price; otherwise *murabaha* should not, in principle, be under suspicion for it is a universally recognized concept under Islamic law.

There are two aspects with regard to the implementation of the concept of *murabaha* which are of interest to the present study and which are settled in different fashions by the various schools of law. These aspects are:

(a) What sort of expenses incurred subsequent to his purchase would a *murabaha* vendor be allowed to add to the *murabaha* price?
(b) What options are open to a *murabaha* purchaser if he discovers that the *murabaha* price was unduly inflated?

Expenses in relation to *murabaha*

For the Malikis, expenses which can be added to the capital (price) and constitute a basis for the calculation of the profit are those which have affected the commodity itself, such as dying or tailoring a piece of material. Expenses which, although added to the capital, cannot serve for the calculation of the profit, are those which did not affect the commodity itself and which were incurred for services that the *murabaha* vendor could not provide personally, such as the fare for transporting or storing the commodities in a warehouse or in a storage place rented for the purpose. Finally, there are expenses which can neither be added to the capital nor taken into account for the calculation of the profit; these are expenses which do not affect the commodity itself and which furthermore are incurred for services

25 Ibrahim Kamel in *Islamic Banks and Strategies of Economic Co-operation*, pp. 65–6.
26 M. Siddiqi, *Issues in Islamic Banking*, pp. 49 and 137ff.

that the *murabaha* vendor is in a position to render personally, such as commissions paid to a middle man or wages for folding pieces of material and so on.[27]

Hanbalis deem that all actual expenses incurred as regards the commodity, the object of the *murabaha*, can be added to the capital (price), provided that the *murabaha* purchaser is made aware of the amount of these expenses and their origins.[28] Similar is the teaching of the Ibadis, who emphasize that all expenses, whether or not they have affected the very object of the *murabaha*, should be stated separately from the price itself.[29]

Shafii teaching, in that respect, is similar to the Hanbali and Ibadi ones, with the requirement that the fee earned, in principle, by the vendor, or the fee which should have been paid to a third party, had he not volunteered to perform a work gratis, cannot be added to the *murabaha* price unless that is specifically accepted by the purchaser.[30]

Hanafis have a different approach to the problem. For them the *murabaha* vendor is entitled to add to the price (capital) all expenses accepted normally by commercial practice and incurred as regards the commodity object of the *murabaha*, whether such expenses have affected the commodity itself (e.g. dying or tailoring a piece of material) or were incurred on account of such commodity (e.g. transporting goods, feeding animals or paying a commission to a middle man).[31]

Options when *murabaha* price proves to be inflated

In the event of a *murabaha* purchaser discovering that the price he has paid to the *murabaha* vendor was unduly inflated, what are the remedies available to him? Abu Hanifa taught that in such a case the purchaser would have to make up his mind either to accept the sale at the stated price or to rescind it and take back his money, but if the purchaser is not longer in possession of the *murabaha* object he would have no other option than to confirm the sale.[32] Some Hanafi learned men such as Abu Yusuf held that the purchaser is, in any circumstances, entitled to confirm the *murabaha* and claim back the undue increase. This is also Ibn Abi Layla's teaching.[33] al-Shammakhi, the Ibadi scholar, wrote that if the price is unduly inflated the buyer would have the option either to confirm the *murabaha* at the stated price or to rescind the contract and have his money back. But in the event of the *murabaha* object being no longer in the buyer's possession, then the sale stands and the buyer has no other option.[34]

27 Ibn Rushd, *Bidayat al-mujtahid*, Vol. II, p. 214.
28 Ibn Qudama, *al-Mughni*, Vol. IV, p. 201.
29 al-Shammakhi, *al-Idah*, Vol. III, pp. 490–1.
30 Jaziri, *al-Fiqh 'ala al-madhahib*, Vol. II, p. 280.
31 Ibid., p. 281.
32 Ibid., pp. 281–2.
33 Ibid; al-Shafi'i, *al-Umm*, Vol. III, p. 93.
34 al-Shammakhi, *al-Idah*, Vol. III, pp. 494–5.

The Maliki view granted the *murabaha* purchaser an option, but a qualified one. This purchaser would have the right either to keep the *murabaha* object in consideration of its real cost plus price (i.e. the price after devaluation of the undue increase) or to relinquish the object of the transaction, unless the *murabaha* vendor forces him to keep it at the cost plus price.[35]

The Shafii teaching, with regard to this particular matter, was that if the *murabaha* object is still in the *murabaha* buyer's possession, he is then entitled to give it back to the vendor and have his money in return, or he can keep it and claim the undue increase; otherwise he is entitled to request from the *murabaha* vendor payment of the undue increase.[36] However, Ibn Rushd[37] has attributed to the Shafii teaching in this respect two different versions. The first says that the *murabaha* purchaser is forced to keep the *murabaha* object after the undue increase is rebated. The second version accords with the teaching of Ahmad Ibn Hanbal.[38]

Ijara

Ijara means a lease contract as well as a hire contract. In the context of Islamic banking it is a lease contract under which the bank or financial institution leases equipment or a building to one of its clients against a fixed charge. The different schools of law whose work is discussed in this book give practically the same definitions of *ijara*.

For the Maliki Ibn Rushd *ijara* resembles a sale contract whereby the price and use (*manfaʿa*) are exchanged.[39] Use should be determined either by the duration of the contract or by its subject-matter. Furthermore, the use should be lawful and not a mandatory duty.[40] Thus, renting premises for their use as a cabaret is invalid, for the purpose of the contract is illicit; and hiring a mother to feed her own baby is invalid, for it is her mandatory duty to do so. The Hanbali al-Bahuti has described *ijara* as being a contract where the subject-matter is the lawful and defined use (*manfaʿa*), of a lawful and determined corporeal object (*ʿayn*), for a specific period of time. It is also a contract for providing a defined work for a fixed price.[41] Hanafi *ijara* is a contract intended to give ownership of a determined and legitimate use (*manfaʿa*) of a rented corporeal object (*ʿayn*) against a consideration.[42] For the Shafiis, *ijara* is a contract where the subject-matter is the determined,

35 Ibn Rushd, *Bidayat al-mujtahid*, Vol. II, p. 215.
36 al-Shafiʿi, *al-Umm*, Vol. III, p. 93.
37 Ibn Rushd, *Bidayat al-mujtahid*, Vol. II, p. 215.
38 Ibid; Jaziri, *al-Fiqh ʿala al-madhahib*, Vol. II, p. 283; Ibn Qudama, *al-Mughni*, Vol. IV, p. 199.
39 Ibn Rushd, *Bidayat al-mujtahid*, Vol. II, pp. 219–20.
40 Ibn Juzay, *Qawanin*, p. 302.
41 al-Bahuti *al-Rawd al-murbiʿ*, p. 214.
42 Jaziri, *al-Fiqh ʿala al-madhahib*, Vol. III, p. 94.

legitimate, assignable and lawful use of an object against a fixed consideration.[43] Finally, the Ibadis see *ijara* as a sort of sale of the use but not of the corporeal object[44] from which that use is derived.

These definitions indicate that *ijara* is a bilateral contract where the use of a corporeal object is exchanged for a price. The rules for averting *riba* apply to *ijara*, and these rules, as we have previously seen, vary from one school of law to another. We have also seen (pp. 54ff. above) that with *ijara* the subject-matter materializes gradually by the lessee making use of a hired object and that is a tolerated exception to the requirement that a subject-matter should be in existence at the time the contract is concluded. That requirement cannot be met when work or use is the subject-matter; the latter is necessarily non-existent at the time the contract is concluded but comes progressively into being by the gradual implementation of the contract. Equity (*istihsan*), necessity (*darura*) and the Prophet's precedents have lead to the toleration of *ijara*, provided no room is left for a material want of knowledge (*jahl*), which may develop into a dispute.

The concept of *ijara* was examined in great detail by *fiqh* (jurisprudence). Here we select one aspect which can have an important bearing on future relations between banks and their clients: Muslim scholars had lengthy discussions on whether *ijara* is a binding (*lazim*) contract or a non-mandatory (*ja'iz*) one i.e. a contract which can be cancelled virtually at will by either of the contracting parties with no regard to the duration of work agreed in the contract. The vast majority of these scholars have settled for *ijara* being a binding (*lazim*) contract, as did Malik, Shafiʿi, Abu Hanifa and Ibn Hanbal, whereas the Ibadi al-Shammakhi, did not take sides over this question.[45] Even though the four orthodox schools of law are in agreement about *ijara*'s attributes, they disagree about the reasons which could cause the termination of *ijara*. Malikis and Shafiis[46] taught that *ijara* is cancelled only by a material defect (*ʿayb*) affecting the corporeal object (*ʿayn*) leased or hired, and also if the purpose of the lease or hire has disappeared, such as when a person asks a dentist to remove a painful tooth, and before the operation can be performed the pain disappears. Abu Hanifa[47] said that *ijara* is cancelled by any reasonable excuse that the lessee may invoke. Hanbalis[48] say that *ijara* is cancelled if the rented object is destroyed or affected by a material defect. Ibadis[49] tend to say that the consequence of considering *ijara* as a binding contract means that it cannot be terminated except by what amounts to *force majeure*.

[43] Ibid., p. 98.
[44] al-Shammakhi, *al-Idah*, Vol. III, pp. 556, 562 and 563.
[45] al-Shammakhi, *al-Idah*, Vol. III, pp. 566–7.
[46] Ibn Rushd, *Bidayat al-mujtahid*, Vol. II, p. 229.
[47] Jaziri, *al-Fiqh ʿala al-madhahib*, Vol. III, pp. 154ff.
[48] al-Bahuti, *al-Rawd al-murbiʿ*, p. 217.
[49] al-Shammakhi, *al-Idah*, Vol. III, p. 567.

Ijara wa-iqtina'

This is the hire purchase concept, called by the Islamic financial institutions "lease-purchase financing". It is a combination of leasing movable or immovable properties with granting the lessee an option of eventually acquiring the object of the lease. *Ijara wa-iqtina'* was unknown to traditional Muslim scholars, yet there is nothing unlawful or suspicious in the combination of two well-established concepts, i.e. lease and option, provided that *riba* is avoided and is not what the contracting parties eventually aim at. Islamic institutions aim to make use of *ijara wa-iqtina'* in the following manner. The financial institution will rent a movable or immovable property (e.g. equipment, building etc.) to one of its clients, who will have to pay an agreed sum by instalments over an agreed period into a savings account held with the same financial institution. These instalments are invested in *mudaraba* venture(s) for the client's account. Capital and profit will eventually allow the client to offset the rental cost and to purchase the rented property, unless he decides not to acquire the rented property. In the latter circumstance what remains of the profit, after rental cost and expenses are rebated, is remitted to the client, and the rented property is taken back by the financial institution.

Qard hasan

Qard hasan means an interest-free loan, which is the only loan permitted by Sharia principles. We have seen previously that not only can interest not be charged on the lent capital, but no advantage whatsoever should be derived by the lender from the loan. Of course each school of law has its own interpretation of what constitutes "advantage", and that we have already seen in detail (pp. 41ff. above).

One may wonder how lending could be a business proposition once interest is abolished. It seems that the Islamic financial institutions are advised to make use of *qard hasan* in the following circumstances.

(a) In the case of *musharaka* (partnership or participation financing) between the institution and the client, it often happens that not all of the institution's shares in the project can be earmarked for the right to participate in profits; otherwise no substantial share would be left to the other partner, namely the client. Therefore the institution's participation is split into two parts: one constitutes a share in the partnership capital and the other is working capital provided through *qard hasan*.

(b) A *qard hasan* can also be provided to a client of the institution who has cash-flow problems, either in order to protect the institution's investment, or, when the client is reliable, to boost the institution's image and reputation at no great risk.

(c) A third use of *qard hasan* may occur when a client who has with the financial institution a blocked savings account which generates no interest, encounters an urgent need for short-term finance, making recourse to the *mudaraba* concept useless. The necessary funds can be provided to him by the institution through *qard hasan*. There are probably other circumstances where *qard hasan* has its value for the lender; these circumstances will gradually develop with the day-to-day business of the Islamic financial institutions.

Takaful

Takaful literally means "mutual guarantee". In the context it is the Islamic answer to the modern concept of insurance, which is one of the most controversial subjects among scholars. Some authors see nothing unlawful in the basic principles underlying insurance. For them, insurance is free from gambling and can be freed from interest: furthermore any want of knowledge (*jahl*) and uncertainty (*gharar*) involved are not of a degree large enough to call for its prohibition.[50] Some other authors agree with this view so far as general insurance is concerned but not for life assurance, which in their view is totally unacceptable, for it involves gambling and uncertainty, and goes against the Islamic conception of predestination (*qadar*). Finally, there are some scholars who find an element of gambling in all kinds of insurance as a matter of principle, in addition to the *riba* and *gharar* which are inalienably associated with insurance.[51]

In view of these controversial opinions an alternative was found. Muslims are offered the concept of *takaful* (mutual guarantee) or solidarity *mudaraba* (or solidarity trust), which works in the following manner. The participant in a given solidarity *mudaraba* pays annually an agreed sum of money which remains his property. After a relatively short period of time during which the funds are frozen he can withdraw, at will, from the solidarity *mudaraba* and receive his capital plus the profits accumulated until that date. As long as he remains participating in the solidarity *mudaraba*, his money and that of other participants are invested in *mudaraba* venture(s), or possibly in some other structure valid by Sharia standards, and the profits, if any, distributed to the participants after deduction of the amount of the annual premium. The purpose of this solidarity *mudaraba* may be life assurance and it may also be risk insurance covering a property. If the assured person dies before the end of his covered time, or if an insured risk on the property materializes, then payment is made out of the account of the insured person; if there is not enough money in that account, the outstanding balance is covered by the money of other participants inside the same pool. This is what is meant here by solidarity; the participants in a solidarity *mudaraba* share the consequences of a mishap.[52] In other words, the participants in a given solidarity *madaraba* have the right to share the surplus

[50] M. N. Siddiqi, *Muslim Economic Thinking*, p. 26.
[51] Ibid.
[52] Ibrahim Kamel, *Islamic Banks*, pp. 63–4.

profits generated by such a *mudaraba* but at the same time they are liable for contributing to amounts in addition to the premiums they have already disbursed, if their initial premiums paid in during a particular year are not sufficient to meet all the losses and risks incurred during that year.

3 The *mudaraba* (commenda partnership)

The main objectives of an interest-free bank, as seen by most contemporary Muslim authors and thinkers, are to mobilize funds from the public on the basis of *mudaraba* partnerships and to provide funds to entrepreneurs, essentially on the same basis. In this manner the principal source of income of an interest-free bank will be the difference between the share of profit it receives from the entrepreneurs and the share of profit it gives to the depositors.[53] In order to perform its function, an interest-free bank will enter into a *mudaraba* partnership with the depositor and into a separate one with the entrepreneur. This was called by Muslim economists a two-tier *mudaraba*; it is in fact two separate *mudarabas* with one common party, i.e. the bank, either being directly involved in the operations or acting through a subsidiary.

Ideally, interest-free banks relying on the concept of *mudaraba* should be in a position to deal with pure commercial banking and investment banking, the main source of their revenues, in addition to development banking. If this combination is not legally possible within the existing banking system, then accommodation should be found, probably by resorting to exemptions and special concessions or to the setting up of financial institutions controlled by interest-free banks and enjoying much more flexibility and potential than the banks themselves. There are many capitalist countries which allow commercial banks to sell investment certificates. Some of the drawbacks which this method presents are that the controlling bank would be deprived of a direct main source of revenue and that its scope of activity would be very much confined to basic banking services. This negative aspect, and other peculiarities of the interest-free system relying on the concept of *mudaraba*, have not escaped Muslim financiers and bankers who advocate a drastic change in the organization of the existing banking system in order to make room for the system they promote.[54] Most of them have no illusions about the difficulties of winning the much-needed opening through graceful consent, and work hard to spread and consolidate the rediscovered proposition, "propagating their potentially revolutionary message with the utmost gentility", as it was sharply noted by one expert.[55] The task of the newcomers is made easier by the wealth they enlist, which provides them

[53] Afzallur Rahman, *Banking and Insurance*, p. 333.

[54] Ibid., pp. 336ff.

[55] R. Cooper, "A calculator in one hand and the Koran in the other", *Euromoney*, issue of November 1981, pp. 44ff.

with good listeners eager to co-operate, and also by the unshakeable conviction which is a believer's privilege.

Whether the *mudaraba* is managed by an interest-free bank or by an investment company, the investor will have a choice; he can invest in general investment *mudarabas* organized for general purposes of profitability or in a specific-purpose *mudaraba* such as one for building a factory or a school. In the former case the bank has the right to determine the fields and methods of investment and from the outset the investor, i.e. the client, is asked to sign a document for that purpose. Islamic banks will also control parallel pools, and surplus funds from one pool can be moved to another pool in identical conditions provided the investment is not specifically designed for one project. Duration of a specific-purpose *mudaraba* will be limited to the duration of the specific project or business for which the *mudaraba* was organized, whereas general investment *mudarabas* can have a specific or indefinite duration.

Certificates can be issued in negotiable form, either registered or bearer. Certificates can mature at a fixed date, at a fixed interval after issue, or at call or at a fixed interval after call. Normally *mudaraba* certificates representing interests in a specific-purpose *mudaraba* will mature only upon the termination of the *mudaraba*. *Mudaraba* certificates can be distributed in an underwriting or sales effort of a fixed duration, or be continuously available, or available on a periodic basis. Exact design of the conditions of a *mudaraba* certificate is highly dependent on the nature of the economy in which the *mudaraba* proposes to invest. *Mudaraba* certificates continuously offered and subject to redemption on demand are appropriate only where *mudaraba* assets may be invested to a significant degree in markets providing the necessary depth and liquidity to ensure accurate daily or periodic valuation of assets, and the possibility of sale of assets in organized markets to obtain funds necessary to meet demands for redemption.[56]

Mudaraba is also the vehicle operated by interest-free banks or financial investment companies for supplying clients with funds. In this instance, *mudaraba* is entirely managed by the client, while the profits are distributed amongst the two parties to the *mudaraba* according to the agreed ratio. In that instance the agent-manager, i.e. the client, is bound by the terms of a restricted *mudaraba*, and most of the banks require from him a collateral to guarantee good management and compliance with the terms of the *mudaraba*.

From what has been said, it will be obvious that a proper examination of certain aspects of the *mudaraba* is needed. Advertising prospectuses and introductory literature in circulation today, except for few exceptions, do not provide much legal background; we are not really informed about the legal definition of *mudaraba*; what can constitute a *mudaraba* capital; what

[56] One of the brochures circulated by Dar al Maal al Islami.

are the rights and duties of the parties to a *mudaraba* and how are the affairs of a *mudaraba* liquidated when no contractual agreement to that effect exists, and finally do the schools of law under our scrutiny have the same answer to all these questions? The last part of the present book is intended to deal with these topics.

Definition

Nearly all schools of law have understood *mudaraba* in the following sense: "A contract between at least two parties whereby one party, called the investor (*rabb al-mal*) entrusts money to the other party called the agent-manager (*mudarib*) who is to trade with it in an agreed manner and then return to the investor the principal and a pre-agreed share of the profits and keep for himself what remains of such profits." The division of profits between the two parties must necessarily be on a proportional basis and cannot be a lump sum or a guaranteed return. In a valid *mudaraba* the investor is not liable for losses beyond the amount of the capital he has paid. Conversely the agent-manager, who does not normally partake in the investment in terms of money, does not bear any share of the losses, losing only his time and effort.

The Islamic financial institutions have adopted a different terminology when referring to *mudaraba* in the English language. *Mudaraba* is called "trust financing", the investor becomes the "beneficial owner" or the "sleeping partner", and the agent-manager is named the "managing trustee" or the "labour partner". I have chosen to use the conventional names in English, i.e. "commenda", "investor" and "agent-manager". The "Société en commandite simple", one of the types of commercial companies adopted by French law, seems directly derived from the mediaeval Western commenda, which in turn has its most probable origin in the Islamic *mudaraba*. By one of those strokes of chance that only can be rationalized afterwards, a more or less French-inspired "Commandite simple" was introduced into the legal system of many Arab countries, such as Lebanon, Oman, Saudi Arabia, the Yemen Arab Republic and others, during the nineteenth and twentieth centuries, through Egyptian and Lebanese draftsmen.

The reintroduced type of commenda or "commandite simple" was not really popular in business circles, they preferred to conduct their business activities through the vehicle of two other types of company, namely the limited liability company (another French-inspired concept, known as the société à responsabilité limitée) and the joint stock company. The reintroduced "commenda" or "société en commandite simple" was mostly used as a family partnership, especially when a widow, children under age or incapacitated persons were among the partners. New interest in commenda, not the "commandite simple" of the commercial laws but the *mudaraba* of

Islamic Sharia, has arisen recently, owing to revival of Sharia in transactions and to the choice made by Islamic financial institutions of *mudaraba* as the main vehicle for mobilizing funds from the public and providing facilities to entrepreneurs. The reason why *mudaraba* was chosen for this is that it represents a happy combination of financial means and human resources within the accepted Sharia standards. True, *mudaraba* capital not accompanied by labour is expected to be rewarded, but this is because it is a risk capital in the sense that the investor has accepted the risk of a business venture. If such a venture is a success he will recover his capital and a pre-agreed proportional share of the profits; if, on the contrary, the venture is unsuccessful, the investor may lose all or part of his investment. Activity undertaken by the agent-manager and risk taken by the investor are their respective justification for sharing in the profits returned by a given *mudaraba*. In the event that the agent-manager is prevented from performing his normal duties as a result of restrictions imposed by the investor, such restrictions are considered null and void. Conversely, in the event that the investor requires the agent's guarantee against the eventuality that the investment is lost in part or totally, such an investment does not qualify as a commenda contract. *Mudaraba* is necessarily a combination of a measure of business activity conducted according to the customary practice of the merchants and a measure of commercial risk taken by the capitalist.

For the Malikis[57] and Shafiis,[58] *mudaraba* activity is necessarily limited to mere trading and to activities ancillary to trade. It cannot involve a manufacturing function on the part of the agent, otherwise it would be considered as a contract of manufacture or hire. Hanafis, on the other hand, see no objection to a *mudaraba* whereby capital is associated with crafts or manufacturing activities such as is the case, for example, when the agent is entrusted with a capital fund in cash on the condition that he will have to buy raw materials and turn them into finished products and then sell them on the basis of a profit-sharing *mudaraba*.[59] Hanbalis, apparently, allow the investor and the agent-manager to enter into two separate contracts, one of manufacture and one of *mudaraba*, provided that one is not a condition for the other.[60] Ibadis, on the contrary, do not allow the co-existence of *mudaraba* with a hire contract or indeed with any other sort of contract.[61]

Mudaraba capital

All schools of law agree that dinars (gold currency) and dirhams (silver currency) are valid *mudaraba* investment forms. Controversy among them

57 Ibn Juzay, *Qawanin*, p. 309.
58 al-Nawawi, *Minhaj al-talibin* (trans. E. C. Howard), p. 210.
59 al-Sarakhsi, *al-Mabsut*, Vol. XXII, p. 54.
60 Ibn Qudama, *al-Mughni*, Vol. V, pp. 27–8.
61 al-Shammakhi, *al-Idah*, Vol. IV, p. 9.

concerns unminted gold and silver as well as *fulus* (token copper coins). This has no real interest to us, for the reason that practically speaking all countries nowadays deal with all known major currencies often within mandatory rules and principles set up by each country. However, other points, amply discussed by traditional Muslim scholars, are still of interest. One of them concerns chattels (*ʿurud*). Finding out whether or not a *mudaraba* can be formed with chattels (*ʿurud*) as an investment is of importance in view of the revival of the *mudaraba* concept.

Hanafis,[62] Malikis,[63] Shafiis,[64] Hanbalis[65] and Ibadis[66] deem chattels (*ʿurud*) ineligible for the formation of *mudaraba*. The reason for such rejection lies in the fact that the price of chattels may well fluctuate between the date they are remitted to the agent-manager and the date of their conversion into ready money. This risk renders the *mudaraba* subject-matter undefined and undetermined, in addition to the fact that the *mudaraba* starting-point is also uncertain, for it is not known beforehand when ready money will be available. This involves a sufficiently strong element of *gharar* to lead to a dispute, and it was therefore denied that chattels were a valid *mudaraba* investment. However, there is a qualification to the unanimity shown by the schools of law. Hanafi[67] and Hanbali[68] teachings allow the setting up of a *mudaraba* with the proceeds of the sale of specifically designated chattels once they are sold, but not before. In that way the capital on hand is the price and not the chattels. The Hanafi and Hanbali permissive view in this instance relies on their teaching that a *mudaraba* may be made contingent upon the fulfilment of a pre-condition, which is in the present case the sale of the chattels (*ʿurud*); once the chattels are sold the investment form is duly determined with no risk or uncertainty.

Malikis, Shafiis, Hanafis,[69] Hanbalis[70] and Ibadis[71] disallow the setting up of a *mudaraba* by way of the creditor asking his debtor to consider the debt owed to him as a *mudaraba* investment, for this could enable the creditor to obtain an illegitimate advantage out of a loan and also, according to al-Shafiʿi and Abu Hanifa, a debt owed by a *dhimma*[72] cannot be transformed into a fiduciary relationship (*amana*) which is the ascribed relationship of the two parties to a contract of *mudaraba*. Is the outcome still the same if the creditor appoints an agent with the aim of collecting a debt from a third party

62 al-Sarakhsi, *al-Mabsut*, Vol. XXII, p. 33.
63 Ibn Rushd, *Bidayat al-mujtahid*, Vol. II, pp. 236–7.
64 al-Shirbini, *Mughni al-muhtaj*, Vol. II, p. 310.
65 Jaziri, *al-Fiqh ʿala al-madhahib*, Vol. III, p. 43.
66 al-Shammakhi, *al-Idah*, Vol. IV, pp. 7–8.
67 Ibn Rushd, *Bidayat al-mujtahid*, Vol. II, p. 237.
68 Jaziri, *al-Fiqh ʿala al-madhahib*, Vol. III, p. 43.
69 Ibn Rushd, *Bidayat al-mujtahid*, Vol. II, p. 237.
70 Ibn Qudama, *al-Mughni*, Vol. V, p. 73.
71 al-Shammakhi, *al-Idah*, Vol. IV, p. 8.
72 For the two meanings of *dhimma* see p. 81 above.

and of considering it, once collected, as a *mudaraba* investment? Hanbalis,[73] Hanafis and one opinion attributed to al-Shafiʿi[74] have no objection to that, whereas Malikis,[75] Ibadis[76] and another opinion attributed to al-Shafiʿi[77] do not allow it, for it adds to the burden of the agent-manager or secures to the investor an extra advantage which is neither part of the capital nor a share of the profits and therefore illegitimate.

Investor's duties and rights

Investor's duty to hand over the *mudaraba* investment. Practically speaking, the sole duty of the investor is to hand over the *mudaraba* capital to the agent-manager; otherwise the contemplated *mudaraba* would be invalid.[78] However, the initial act of trading is sufficient to put the operation into force, without making the contract, at any stage, a binding (*lazim*) one.[79] Conversely, the investor has the right to have his investment back out of the net proceeds of the *mudaraba* liquidation, once it is completed by the agent-manager and to the extent that such proceeds permit. The investor cannot request the agent's guarantee for the return of the investment: such a condition is deemed null and void. But the *mudaraba* contract itself remains valid, according to Ibn Hanbal and Abu Hanifa[80] whereas, according to Malik and al-Shafiʿi[81] the *mudaraba* contract as a whole is invalid. The latter is also the Ibadi teaching.[82]

73 Ibn Qudama, *al-Mughni*, Vol. v, p. 74.

74 Ibn Rushd, *Bidayat al-mujtahid*, Vol. ii, p. 237.

75 Ibid.

76 al-Shammakhi, *al-Idah*, Vol. iv, pp. 8–9.

77 Jaziri, *al-Fiqh ʿala al-madhahib*, Vol. iii, p. 48.

78 al-Sarakhsi, *al-Mabsut*, Vol. xxii, p. 84; al-Zurqani, *Sharh al-Muwatta'*, Vol. iii, p. 347; Ibn Qudama, *al-Mughni*, Vol. v, p. 29; al-Nawawi, *Minhaj al-talibin* (trans. E. C. Howard), p. 210; al-Shammakhi, *al-Idah*, Vol. iv, note on p. 6.

79 The question of the creation of legal relations is treated by Sharia as distinct from the question of the completion of such relations. For instance if it is intended by a transaction to effect a transfer of a physical object, the legal relations in such a case will not, strictly speaking, be said to be completed until the transfer has actually taken place (for more detail see Abdur Rahim, *Muhammadan Jurisprudence*, pp. 282ff.). Other types of contract, such as *mudaraba* and partnership in general, can be terminated by the will of either of the contracting parties at any point and without constituting a breach of contract.

These peculiarities of the law of contract as taught by *fiqh* have incited some authors to write that "in Muhammadan law, contract, with some apparent exceptions such as agency and suretyship, remains a branch of conveyance; and the step forward from a completed transfer to a legally binding promise has not been taken". (Seymour Vesey-Fitzgerald, *Muhammadan Law*, pp. 181–2).

80 Ibn Qudama, *al-Mughni*, Vol. v, p. 68.

81 Ibn Rushd, *Bidayat al-mujtahid*, Vol. ii, p. 238.

82 al-Shammakhi, *al-Idah*, Vol. iv, p. 11.

Investor's right to see the agent complying with the terms of the *mudaraba*. The reason for the unacceptability of the agent's guarantee is that such an agent, likewise any partner, is considered a trustworthy party (*amin*) with respect to the capital remitted to him. He is therefore not liable for any loss occurring in the normal course of the business activities, except when there is a breach of trust. A typical example of this is when the agent-manager breaks one or more of the agreed or implied *mudaraba* conditions[83] and infringes what is recognized as the investor's right to see the agent-manager discharge his duties pursuant to the specifically agreed terms of the *mudaraba* or, in the absence of such terms, pursuant to the provisions of the law governing that *mudaraba*.

The implied *mudaraba* conditions vary from one school of law to another; moreover, they do not stem from the general *mudaraba* theories as outlined above, but are found instead in a considerable number of cases, whether real or theoretical, discussed by various traditional scholars. Nevertheless, if we follow a reverse course of investigations – that is, if we proceed from the cases treated by the scholars, certain guidelines may be derived, as follows.

The legitimacy of the agent's conduct is determined by comparing his questioned action with the customary practice of the merchants. If such action is in conformity with that practice then it is deemed legitimate and binding upon the investor unless it contravenes any of the specifically pre-agreed terms of the *mudaraba*. This criterion is the one adopted by all the schools of law within the present study,[84] save for the Shafii school which has advocated a slightly different rule, albeit with not very different implications. The Shafii rule is that the agent-manager, when administering the *mudaraba* affairs, should act as any prudent man would act under the circumstances.[85] (This is strikingly similar to the comparatively modern French criterion of *le bon père de famille*.)

Granted the virtual unanimity of the schools of law in selecting this criterion, it remains the case that each of these schools has flourished in its own peculiar environment and economic ambience, with the consequence that customary practice differs from one place to another. The immediate result is that the powers of an agent-manager, acting pursuant to a *mudaraba* governed by Hanafi teaching, for example, are not the same as those of an agent-manager operating a *mudaraba* established under a different Islamic teaching. It would be too tedious to enumerate all the differences found among the powers enjoyed by various agents acting under differently governed *mudarabas*. What we can do is to illustrate the position by a typical

[83] Ibn Qudama, *al-Mughni*, Vol. v, p. 54; al-Shafi'i, *al-Umm*, Vol. II, p. 10; al-Zurqani, *Sharh al-Muwatta'*, Vol. III, pp. 354–5; Jaziri, *al-Fiqh 'ala al-madhahib*, Vol. III, p. 51; al-Basyani, *Mukhtasar*, p. 309; al-Shammakhi, *al-Idah*, Vol. IV, p. 12.

[84] al-Sarakhsi, *al-Mabsut*, Vol. XXII, p. 47; Ibn Rushd, *Bidayat al-mujtahid*, Vol. II, p. 242; al-Shammakhi, *al-Idah*, Vol. IV, p. 15; Ibn Qudama, *al-Mughni*, Vol. v, p. 56.

[85] al-Nawawi, *Minhaj al-talibin* (trans. E. C. Howard), p. 212.

example, such as the sale of *mudaraba* properties performed on credit by an agent-manager not empowered to do so by specific instructions. For the Hanafis[86] and Hanbalis[87] the agent-manager is entitled, in the absence of any instructions to the contrary, to sell *mudaraba* properties on credit. Shafiis,[88] Malikis[89] and Ibadis[90] deny the agent-manager that right.

Investor's right to share in the profits. Another right recognized to belong to the investor is that of sharing in the profits. Such a share should be determined on a strictly proportional basis, otherwise the commenda partnership is invalid.[91] One violation frequently discussed in the sources is when either of the parties stipulates, as his expected return, a specific sum of money instead of, or in addition to, a proportional share of the profits. Such an arrangement is also invalid owing to the strong element of *gharar* (risk, speculation, uncertainty) it contains. This is because the future existence of the promised lump sum was very uncertain when the promise was made, and furthermore its actual ratio to the real profit was totally unknown. Another reason for the illegality of such an arrangement is that it is not the business risk which is rewarded but the mere act of remitting money to the agent-manager. That amounts to a *ribawi* transaction.

What is the position when either the investor or the agent-manager is allocated all the profits? Malikis[92] have no objection to either prospect; it is deemed by them as a gift with no adverse bearing on the *mudaraba*. That is not the case for the Shafiis[93] and Hanbalis,[94] who consider that any clause securing for the investor or the agent-manager all the profits renders the *mudaraba* invalid, for it conflicts with the objectives and the essence of the concept of *mudaraba*, which necessarily entail the distribution of the profits between the two contracting parties. Hanafis[95] and most Ibadis[96] share the following view on the matter: when all the profits are to go to the agent-manager, the contract which contains such a clause is no longer a contract of *mudaraba* but a contract of loan (*qard*). In such a contract the borrower (i.e. the agent-manager in the abortive *mudaraba*) is liable to refund to the lender (i.e. the investor in the abortive *mudaraba*) the equivalent or the like of what

86 Jaziri, *al-Fiqh ʿala al-madhahib*, Vol. III, p. 53.
87 Ibn Qudama, *al-Mughni*, Vol. V, p. 40.
88 Ibn Rushd, *Bidayat al-mujtahid*, Vol. II, p. 242.
89 Ibid.
90 al-Shammakhi, *al-Idah*, Vol. IV, pp. 24–6.
91 al-Sarakhsi, *al-Mabsut*, Vol. XXII, pp. 22ff.; al-Zurqani, *Sharh al-Muwatta'*, Vol. III, pp. 349–50; al-Haythami, *al-Fatawa*, Vol. III, p. 111; al-Shammakhi, *al-Idah*, Vol. IV, p. 13; Ibn Qudama, *al-Mughni*, Vol. V, p. 38.
92 Ibn Rushd, *Bidayat al-mujtahid*, Vol. II, p. 238; Ibn Qudama, *al-Mughni*, Vol. V, p. 35.
93 al-Haythami, *al-Fatawa*, Vol. III, p. 111; Ibn Qudama, *al-Mughni*, Vol. V, p. 35.
94 Ibn Qudama, *al-Mughni*, Vol. V, p. 35.
95 Ibn Rushd, *Bidayat al-mujtahid*, Vol. II, p. 238; Ibn Qudama, *al-Mughni*, Vol. V, p. 35.
96 al-Shammakhi, *al-Idah*, Vol. IV, pp. 10–11.

he has received, whereas he has no such liability under a proper *mudaraba* contract unless it is proven that he has violated the trust bestowed upon him. When the profits are all secured for the advantage of the investor, Hanafis and most Ibadis advocate that the contract is no longer *mudaraba* but an *ibdaʿ*.[97]

Investor's right to a limited liability. Finally the investor has the right to see his liability exclusively limited to the capital he has invested. To protect the investor's interest in this regard, all schools of law placed the same restriction on the agent's activities. He was not permitted to commit the commenda partnership to any sum greater than the capital in hand without the investor's specific authorization. If he exceeded these bounds in any way, the agent became personally liable for any sum in excess of the commenda capital.[98] We have to recall, on this occasion, that Islamic law did not envisage the separation of assets, those of the company and those of the partners, as a way of defining liability among the partners themselves and towards third parties. As a matter of principle, the liability of the partners in all Islamic partnerships, except for the investor in *mudaraba*, is unlimited and "each partner is responsible for his share of the partnership's indebtedness regardless of what it amounts to, or by how much it exceeds the value of his own share of the partnership's assets",[99] notwithstanding a certain number of limitations.[100] The position is not the same when it comes to *mudaraba*, and that probably explains why *mudaraba* was not completely identified with partnerships: once the investor has remitted the *mudaraba* investment to the agent-manager and the latter has carried out the initial act of trading, the investor's financial liability is exhausted; no one has any further claim on him. He is completely screened by the agent-manager, and the latter cannot under normal circumstances compel him to bear any additional financial liability which the investor did not at the start or does not now want to sustain.

Agent-manager's duties and rights

Agent's duty to comply with the terms of the *mudaraba*. The primary duty of the agent-manager is to comply with the trust (*amana*) vested in him while conducting the *mudaraba* affairs. He must follow scrupulously all terms agreed with the investor and if he is faced with a problem for which there are no specific instructions he should follow the customary practice of the mer-

97 *Ibdaʿ* is defined by Article 1059 of the *Majalla* as being the remittance of capital to a person who will trade with it on the understanding that all the profits are for the capitalist. For more detail on *ibdaʿ* see Udovitch, *Partnership and Profit in Medieval Islam* pp. 101ff.

98 Udovitch, *Partnership and Profit*, p. 243.

99 Ibid., p. 41.

100 N. Saleh, *The General Principles of Saudi Arabian and Omani Company Laws*, pp. 105–7.

chants. Such practice is not common to all schools of law, for the reason, as seen earlier, that each of these schools has flourished in a different economic milieu, which has generated a particular business practice. But where all schools of law *are* in agreement is in depriving the agent-manager of authority to borrow money on behalf of the *mudaraba* unless he is specifically authorized to do so by the investor. This prohibition is the normal corollary of the investor's limited liability. Because the investor's liability has a ceiling, which is the precise amount of the *mudaraba* investment, this ceiling cannot be exceeded without the investor's consent, not even for meeting expenses made necessary for the transportation, conservation, transformation or improvement of the *mudaraba* properties. If the agent-manager exceeds the limits of the *mudaraba* investment, without a specific authorization or without a subsequent confirmation, then he is personally liable for the amount of money in excess.[101] This is most probably the only occasion, if we except the case of violation of the trust, when the agent-manager will have to assume personal financial liability with no recourse possible against the investor.

Agent's duty to liquidate the *mudaraba*. Another duty that rests on the agent-manager is to reconvert the *mudaraba* investment to money. That is an important function, for it is only when the *mudaraba* investment is reconverted to its initial state, i.e. money, that the *mudaraba* is considered dissolved and the agent-manager is entitled to appropriate his share of the profits, if any.[102] Moreover, the agent-manager does not enjoy legal possession of his share of the profits (we have to recall that all the profits are normally in his custody), unless it is taken in the investor's presence or with the investor's permission and then only after the initial investment has been fully returned to its owner.[103]

Mudaraba liquidation represents the culmination of the acts of commerce entrusted to the agent-manager, for it is the normal way for achieving a profit with respect to a given venture. It remains to be seen, however, whether *mudaraba* liquidation is always left to the investor's own assessment of the proper time for performing such liquidation, or whether it can be forced upon him at a time he has not chosen or does not favour. There are circumstances where *mudaraba* is terminated *ipso facto*. Such is the case when one of the contracting parties dies or is incapacitated,[104] although it is to be noted that the Malikis do not consider the death of one of the

101 Ibn Rushd, *Bidayat al-mujtahid*, Vol. II, p. 241; Jaziri, *al-Fiqh ʿala al-madhahib*, Vol. III, pp. 53–4; Ibn Qudama, *al-Mughni*, Vol. V, p. 47; al-Shammakhi, *al-Idah*, Vol. IV, pp. 24–6.

102 Ibn Rushd, *Bidayat al-mujtahid*, Vol. II, p. 240.

103 Jaziri, *al-Fiqh ʿala al-madhahib*, Vol. III, pp. 61–2; al-Shammakhi, *al-Idah*, Vol. IV, pp. 27–8; al-Shafiʿi, *al-Umm*, Vol. IV, p. 10; Ibn Qudama, *al-Mughni*, Vol. V, p. 57.

104 al-Nawawi, *Minhaj al-talibin* (trans. E. C. Howard), p. 213; al-Shammakhi, *al-Idah*, Vol. IV, p. 17; al-Salimi, *Jawhar al-nizam* (edn revised by I. Atfish), p. 326; Ibn Qudama, *al-Mughni*, Vol. V, p. 64.

contracting parties to a *mudaraba* as necessarily entailing the end of such *mudaraba*;[105] but this Maliki view is rather isolated from the teaching of other Islamic schools.

Aside from these circumstances, there is a *mudaraba* characteristic which can, theoretically, clash with the recognized right of the agent-manager to decide freely the proper time for bringing the affairs of the *mudaraba* to a prosperous end. This is the fact that a *mudaraba* contract is a non-binding one (*ghayr lazim*) and can therefore be terminated by the will of either party, at any point. The reason is that *mudaraba* is deemed a fiduciary relationship and as such either of the contracting parties involved therein may disengage himself at the moment of his choice, either because he has lost his confidence in the other contracting party or because the latter has violated the trust (*taʿaddin*), or even for no reason at all.

The question is how to reconcile the apparently loose contractual ties created by a *mudaraba* contract with the trading authority bestowed upon the agent-manager, who is expected to generate the maximum profit by deciding precisely when to buy and when to sell the *mudaraba* properties. The potential conflict here did not escape the various schools of law, and they resolved the problem in various ways. Hanbali and Shafii schools teach that if the agent-manager takes the decision to sell the *mudaraba* properties at an expected profit, but the investor tells him not to do so, the agent-manager can disregard the investor's instructions and proceed with the sale. If the sale is to be performed with no expected profit, then the investor is entitled to prevent it. If on the other hand it is the investor who requests the sale and the agent-manager who refuses to perform it, the Shafii school, in its widely taught view, rules that the agent-manager is bound to accept the investor's instructions, despite the absence of profit, whereas the Hanbali school rules that the agent-manager is under an obligation to accept such a sale only if it will generate profit.[106] Hanafis hold the view that once the *mudaraba* investment is transformed into chattels (*ʿurud*), the investor is no longer in a position to prevent the agent-manager from dealing with the *mudaraba* properties as he sees fit.[107] In other words, the investor cannot force the agent-manager to sell the *mudaraba* properties, nor can he prevent him from selling them. Malikis advocate in the above cases that recourse should be made to a third party, more precisely an expert, who will have to say whether it is a suitable time for selling or whether it will be best to wait for a more profitable occasion.[108] The Ibadis seem to class the sale of *mudaraba* properties among the rights of which the investor cannot be deprived, for the reason that the *mudaraba* properties belong to the investor. On the other hand, if it is the agent-manager who has decided to

105 Ibn Juzay *Qawanin*, p. 310.
106 Ibn Qudama, *al-Mughni*, Vol. v, pp. 64–5.
107 al-Sarakhsi, *al-Mabsut*, Vol. xxii, p. 58; S. Baz, *Sharh al-Majalla*, s.v. Article 1420.
108 al-Zurqani, *Sharh al-Muwatta'*, Vol. iii, p. 361.

perform the sale despite the investor's opposition, there is a distinction: if there is no apparent profit then the agent-manager cannot proceed with the sale, but if a profit is expected, then the agent-manager is entitled to perform the transaction despite the investor's opposition.[109]

It appears from the above discussion that *fiqh* endeavours to maintain a balance between three *mudaraba* features, namely (1) the recognized right of both the investor and the agent-manager to cancel the *mudaraba* contract at will; (2) the agent's right not to be deprived of his expected share of the profits notwithstanding the investor's decision to terminate the *mudaraba* prematurely; and finally (3) the investor's expectation of having his investment back, plus his share of the expected profits, should not be foiled by the agent's unilateral decision to withdraw from the *mudaraba* at an improper time. In other words, *mudaraba* is terminated, in normal circumstances, by the agent-manager selling the *mudaraba* properties at an appropriate time and returning to the investor his capital, or such portion of it as was not lost, and distributing the profits, if any, according to the predetermined ratio. In other circumstances, *mudaraba* properties are to be sold after making sure that the sale, if not profitable, brings the lesser harm to both the investor and the agent-manager. This criterion of "the lesser harm" is a controversial matter among the schools of law.

***Mudaraba* with a predetermined duration.** The above guidelines led the Malikis[110] and Shafiis[111] to refuse to recognize the validity of a *mudaraba* with a predetermined duration. This was not the position of the Hanafis[112] and Hanbalis:[113] they tried to reconcile *mudaraba* principles with a predetermined duration, and saw no contradiction between the two. The reasoning they expounded was that both parties to a *mudaraba* are made aware of the fact that their association will necessarily end after the elapse of a fixed period of time; hence they are in a position to take all precautionary measures in order not to be taken by surprise by the deadline's occurrence.

It is worth noting that when a *mudaraba* is of predetermined duration this does not mean that the investor and the agent-manager are precluded from making use of their basic right, that of withdrawing from the *mudaraba* at will; it means only that the agent-manager is not entitled, after the elapse of the pre-agreed duration, to continue performing acts of commerce on behalf of the *mudaraba*, if we except the liquidation itself.

Agent's right to conduct the *mudaraba* affairs with an appropriate degree of freedom. As long as the agent-manager is in charge of the *mudaraba* affairs,

[109] al-Shammakhi, *al-Idah*, Vol. IV, pp. 16–17.
[110] Jaziri, *al-Fiqh 'ala al-madhahib*, Vol. III, p. 41.
[111] Ibid., pp. 45–6.
[112] Ibid., p. 51; also Article 1423 of the *Majalla*.
[113] Ibn Qudama, *al-Mughni*, Vol. V, pp. 69–70.

he is empowered to act with a certain degree of freedom. It is true that the investor, also, has the right to issue instructions and impose restrictions, but that is only to the extent that his instructions, or restrictions, do not grossly hamper or frustrate the purpose of the *mudaraba*, which is to achieve a profit through the acts of commerce performed by the agent-manager. When the investor's instructions or restrictions do have the effect of paralysing the agent's liberty of action or of frustrating the aforesaid purposes, they are considered null and void.

Each of the Islamic schools of law has produced a long list of terms and conditions that the investor might require to form the pattern for the conduct of the *mudaraba* affairs, and each of these conditions and terms was branded either valid or void, depending on the scholar's affiliation to one school or another. It would take too long to reproduce the many cases quoted in the treatises, but what we can do is to illustrate the divergence of these schools by a typical example. The one I have in mind is the matter of the investor participating in works on behalf of the *mudaraba*. Whereas the Hanafis, Malikis and Shafiis[114] deem that any requirement to the effect that the investor is entitled to participate in the *mudaraba* affairs renders that *mudaraba* defective (*fasid*) – although acknowledging the possibility of the investor giving his advice to a reasonable extent – the Hanbalis[115] and Ibadis[116] teach that any prerequisite which empowers the investor to take part in the administration of the *mudaraba* is perfectly valid.

Agent's right to have the expenses deducted from the capital. The agent is given leave to deduct all legitimate business expenses from the investment capital in his trust. The limits of his freedom are defined by its conformity to the twin criteria of customary commercial practice and the pursuit of profit.[117] That is the unanimous teaching of the schools of law discussed in this book. The same consensus is not found when it comes to the agent's personal expenses. On the contrary, the schools of law have dissimilar views which can be summarized as follows.

In a *mudaraba* governed by Hanafi law, the agent-manager is entitled to all his personal expenses provided only that he has spent them while on a journey acting on behalf of the *mudaraba*. It is not necessary that the agent's right be expressly stipulated in the terms of the *mudaraba*, nor it is a prerequisite that the size of the *mudaraba* investments should provide an allowance for the expenses.[118] This is not the case for a *mudaraba* governed by Maliki law, whereby the agent-manager is given leave to take his personal expenses out of the investment, provided that they are incurred during a

114 Jaziri, *al-Fiqh 'ala al-madhahib*, Vol. III, pp. 37, 44 and 45.
115 Ibn Qudama, *al-Mughni*, Vol. V, p. 29.
116 al-Shammakhi, *al-Idah*, Vol. IV, p. 16.
117 Udovitch, *Partnership and Profit*, p. 230.
118 Article 1419 of the *Majalla*.

business journey and provided furthermore that the size of the *mudaraba* investment allows such personal expenses to be deducted therefrom.[119]

A more pragmatic ruling is found in the *mudaraba* governed by Hanbali law, which has left the matter of personal expenses to the understanding of the two contracting parties, allowing great flexibility: personal expenses may be deducted from the *mudaraba* investment, if that is the wish of both parties, whether they are incurred at home or abroad and whether or not the *mudaraba* investment is sufficiently large. All depends on the agreement of the investor and the agent-manager.[120]

It is understood from the conflicting accounts of the Shafii teaching that an agent, in a *mudaraba* governed by Shafii law, is in no position to deduct his personal expenses from the *mudaraba* investment, unless these expenses are incurred during a business journey and unless the investor authorizes him to do so.[121]

Finally, the agent's personal expenses in an Ibadi *mudaraba* can be deducted from the *mudaraba* investment provided that this was agreed with the investor and provided furthermore that the quantum of such expenses is predetermined; that is to say that the agent's deductible expenses should aways be in a pre-agreed lump sum.[122]

The agent's right to share in the profits. The provisions of the *mudaraba* contract regarding the division of profits should be clearly spelled out. One condition found in all schools of law is that the share of the profits, whether for the investor or for the agent, should be determined on a strictly proportional basis, otherwise the *mudaraba* would be invalid.[123]

119 Ibn Rushd, *Bidayat al-mujtahid*, Vol. II, p. 240.

120 Ibn Qudama, *al-Mughni*, Vol. V, p. 70; al-Bahuti, *al-Rawd al-murbiʿ*, p. 211.

121 al-Nawawi, *Minhaj al-talibin* (trans. E. C. Howard), p. 212; Jaziri, *al-Fiqh ʿala al-madhahib*, Vol. III, p. 50; Ibn Qudama, *al-Mughni*, Vol. V, p. 70; Ibn Rushd, *Bidayat al-mujtahid*, Vol. II, p. 240.

122 al-Shammakhi, *al-Idah*, Vol. IV, p. 21.

123 For more detail see pp. 108–9 above.

Conclusion: the unique character of the Sharia Law of Contract and the prospects for success of an Islamic banking system

The Sharia Law of Contract,[1] as viewed by the more permissive schools of law, seems to endorse to a fair extent the expression of the contracting parties' free will but at the same time enjoins the said parties to conform to a predetermined contractual pattern, including a number of mandatory rules and strict prohibitions: it appears to be taking back with one hand what was given by the other. Nevertheless, some modern scholars have attempted to identify the Sharia Law of Contract with the Western philosophical and juridical theory of Freedom of Contract which is the product of (1) the school of Natural Law, with an overall role given to *voluntas*, and (2) canon law, with its tenet that the non-fulfilment of an obligation is a sin. Amazingly, this reconciliation was not attempted by Western scholars, but by modern Muslim legal authors who wrote their treatises at a time when most Arab countries were in a state of decadence and when they felt that the closer they could bring Sharia to Western positive law the better for Sharia. An additional incentive was probably found in the fact that the theory of Freedom of Contract was the cornerstone of nineteenth-century *laissez-faire* economics, which could explain its lasting attraction in societies which have a strong distaste for controlled economics. This trend preceded the actual revival of the Islamic institutions and the uncompromising assertion of their complete autonomy.

Most schools of law teach that in secular matters permissibility is the rule unless there is prohibition; but when this principle is put into practice, these schools have shown a reluctance to allow the contracting parties to a given contract to change the pattern of that contract as defined by Sharia by way of adopting supplemental stipulations which alter its effects.[2] "Permissibility is in any case tempered by a set of requisites which narrow to some extent the avenue open to the contracting parties for deciding unreservedly their terms

[1] "An Islamic law of contracts" is what Noel Coulson rightly considers as a more accurate denomination for the Sharia Law of Contract (N. Coulson, *Commercial Law in the Gulf States*, p. 17).

[2] Supplemental stipulations are technically identified as "Special Conditions" (*shurut*) and were examined in detail earlier (pp. 44ff.).

and conditions. Chief among these requisites is the rule that any given transaction should be devoid of *riba* and *gharar*. We have already seen that *riba* has an ambit much wider than suggested by its inadequate translation into English as "interest" or "usury"; we are also aware now that the prohibition of *gharar* affects all the constitutive elements of a given transaction and compels the contracting parties to have full knowledge or appraisal of the commitments expected to be generated by such transactions.

All these requisites are intended to accompany the inception of secular transactions and to regulate them once in operation, to make sure that neither of the contracting parties suffers wrongs at the time the agreement is reached and furthermore that neither of them will suffer such wrongs during the implementation of the agreement. Actually it is a main concern of the Sharia Law of Contract, if not of the whole Islamic legal system, that no party should be allowed to suffer any undue burden from a given transaction when it is possible with extra care and proper investigation to dispel all risks of *riba* and *gharar*. Once more it is worth stressing that it is not *business risk* which is disallowed but the risk generated by a want of knowledge which materially obscures any of the constitutive elements of a given transaction. It is not the business outcome of such a transaction which needs to be certain, but these elements.

The extra care required by the Sharia Law of Contract during the formative period of a secular transaction as well as the various options (*haqq al-khiyar*)[3] furnished to one or both contracting parties to render the transaction void even after it has been concluded, are the most likely explanation why the concept of lesion[4] (*ghubn*), if not unknown to Sharia, has not particularly recommended itself to Muslim legal scholars. To invalidate a contract impaired by lesion (*ghubn*) is somehow considered an unnecessary remedy: this is because not only are considerable precautionary measures imposed upon the contracting parties in order to make sure that their agreement is devoid of *riba* and *gharar*, and that the promise and the consideration are known and defined to the last detail, but also there are various options available to the contracting parties. If after all these precautions a lesion (*ghubn*) is alleged, that can only mean that the party who suffers from such an unbalanced contract has willingly intended to assume a loss for a reason of his own; therefore this party should not be allowed afterwards to plead the lesion with the aim of rescinding the contract, unless he was incapacitated when he entered the agreement or unless the same lesion has occurred in one of the few transactions that are historically considered as void or was accompanied by misrepresentation.

The legal system based on Sharia is *sui generis* and cannot be confused

[3] See n. 55 on p. 61 above.

[4] The degree of loss, harm or injury sustained by a minor, or person of weak capacity, necessary to entitle him to challenge the transaction by which he suffered the loss.

with other existing systems. Similarities ought to occur between systems of law, and Sharia rules and positive laws may be reconciled, when it comes to secular problems, more frequently than imagined; but it is a perilous and also a sterile exercise systematically to emphasize the resemblances and ignore the differences. With proper means of assessment it becomes clear that more than the concept of Freedom of Contract, it is the requisite that the contractual countervalues should be rated by each contracting party's own assessment as being well balanced, although not necessarily equivalent – except when avoidance of *riba* necessitates – which is the outstanding characteristic of the Islamic Law of Contract. Fairness and good measure in transactions are given more consideration than Freedom of Contract and that is not surprising in a system of law arising out of a religion that is intended to govern the life of the believers in this world in preparation for the world hereafter.

A God-given law has necessarily its set of requisites, abhorrences and ethics that cannot be easily defeated by the mere accord of two persons' wills. By contrast, Western-inspired statutes in effect in Islamic states where Sharia is gaining more ground in the business sphere, do not rely on a background with such restraints. The consequence is that concepts such as Freedom of Contract and Sanctity of Contract are interpreted differently and not accorded the same importance in the one ambience that they have in the other. Which of the two interpretations will prevail cannot be certainly predicted, although all indications for the time being, including the setting up of interest-free banks, point to ultimate victory for Sharia.

It is not unusual to see new ideas – or, as one must say in the present circumstances, ideas revived after being kept in abeyance for a long time – being met by a challenge as soon as they go beyond an abstract stage and begin to be put into practice. The reorganization of the banking system on the basis of Islamic ethics is no exception. The challenge that the reformed institutions confront is not only externally, from the banking and financial systems as still widely practised, but also from within their own ranks. This internal challenge takes the form of some interest-free banks and investment companies resorting, more or less openly, to the use of legal stratagems (*hiyal*) in order to overturn the prohibitions of *riba* and *gharar*. With such means they are in a position to compete, rather unfairly, with other interest-free establishments which confine their activities within more orthodox boundaries.

The consequence, which is not always freely conceded, is that two different operational techniques are current. On the one hand are the bankers and financiers who believe that lawful means can achieve objectives which are not necessarily lawful (that is precisely the objective of a legal stratagem), and who rationalize their technique by the allegation that flexibility will increase the chances of infiltrating the existing system. On the other hand are those who maintain that an Islamic banking system has no *raison d'être* and no prospect for success unless it safeguards the much-heralded legitimacy of its means and objectives; otherwise the whole system will be perverted and its adherents betrayed. What can actually exacerbate the latent conflict between the two operational techniques is their different approaches to the strenuous task which faces all Islamic banks and Investments Companies, namely that of finding further operations and investments which are immune from *riba* and *gharar*. For under a strict interpretation of those two prohibitions, the range of valid transactions is rather limited and the temptation to bend the rules in order to exceed that range is very strong.

It is hard to say, for the moment, whether the two operational techniques will grow up concurrently or whether one technique will eventually prevail over the other. What is certain is that the growing rift which – despite its being played down and despite the fact that opposing views are asserted most of the time with the utmost civility – is in process of splitting the newly established interest-free banking system will do nothing to enhance that system's credibility, and ways must be found to mend the rift.

Glossary

ajal: delay granted to the debtor for the repayment of a loan or for the performance of an obligation.
amāna: fiduciary relationship; deposit on trust; trust.
amīn: trustworthy.
ʿadam: non-existence.
ʿayb: defect.
ʿayn: tangible property right.
ʿamal: work.
ʿāriya: a loan for use only.

bayʿ ghāʾib: sale of what is not visible at the meeting of the parties.
bayʿ juzāf: sale where one of the countervalues is roughly determined by mere viewing.
bayʿ salam: a sale with advance payment for future delivery.
bāṭil: invalid; null and void.
biḍāʿa: commodities.

darak: default in ownership.
ḍarūra: necessity.
ḍarūra muljiʾa or *mulihḥa*: pressing necessity.
dhimma: in Islamic law *dhimma* has two related meanings: from a subjective angle it is the qualification to bear obligations and enjoy rights recognized in each human being by right of birth; it is also from an objective angle the recipient of incorporeal properties.
dīnār: gold currency.
dirham: silver currency.

fals: (token) copper coin.
fāsid: defective; voidable.
faskh: cancellation; termination (of a contract).
fatwā: response on a point of Islamic law issued by a learned man.
fiqh: the science of Islamic law; jurisprudence.

gharar: uncertainty; risk; speculation.
gharar fāḥish: excessive *gharar*.
gharar yasīr: immaterial *gharar*.
ghaṣb: usurpation.
ghayr lāzim: non-binding.
ghubn: damage; injury; fraud; lesion.

ḥadīth: record of actions and sayings of the Prophet.
ḥāja: need.
ḥalāl: lawful.
ḥarām: forbidden; unlawful.
ḥawālat al-dayn: transfer of a debt from one *dhimma* to another *dhimma*.
ḥawālat dayn al-dā'in: assignment of right.
ḥīla: legal stratagem; lawful means used, knowingly and voluntarily, to reach an unlawful objective.

ibdaʿ: remittance of capital for trading on the understanding that profits go to the capitalist.
iflās: bankruptcy.
ijāra: lease contract.
ijāra wa-iqtinā': hire purchase contract; lease-purchase financing.
ijmāʿ: consensus of opinion.
ikrāh: duress; undue influence.
ʿilla: efficient cause.
ʿinan: limited investment partnership.
ʿinan sharikat māl: finance-limited partnership; participation financing.
iqāla: termination of contract by mutual consent.
ʿirbān: see *ʿurbūn*.
iʿsar: insolvency.
istiḥsān: equity.
istiṣnāʿ: contract of manufacture.
ʿitq: manumission of a slave.
ʿiwad: countervalue.

jahl: want of knowledge.
jā'iz: non-mandatory (contract).
jins: genus.
juzāf: see *bayʿ juzāf*.

khiyār: option.
khiyār al-ʿayb: the option on discovery of a defect.
khiyār al-ru'ya: the option after inspection.
khiyār al-waṣf: the option determined by the quality.

lāzim: binding (of a contract).

maḥall: subject-matter.
mahr: dowry, bridal money.
majalla: the Ottoman Civil Code based on Shariʿa, enacted in 1876.
majhūl: unknown.
majlis al-ʿaqd: meeting of the contracting parties.
makrūh: disapproved of; reprehensible.
māl: property; *res in commercio*.
māl mutaqawwam: a corporeal or incorporeal – except for the Hanafis – property with a lawful market price.
māl ribāwī: property susceptible of *riba*.
manfaʿa: use; incorporeal property right.
mashrūʿ: lawful; legitimate.
maysir: game of hazard.
mithlī: a fungible property (an article which is measurable or weighable or accounted by number when alike).
muʿāmala: secular transaction.
muḍāraba: commenda partnership; trust financing.
muḍārib: agent-manager; managing trustee; labour partner.
mufāwaḍa: for the Hanafis and a few other schools of law, an unlimited, unrestricted and equal partnership.
muḥāl ʿalaihi: the new debtor in the *ḥawālat al-dayn*.
muḥāl lahu: creditor-assignee.
muḥarram: forbidden.
muḥīl: debtor-assignor.
munkar: detestable.
murābaḥa: cost-plus-profit contract.
mushāraka: partnership.

nawʿ: species.

qabḍ: possession.
qadar: predestination.
qarḍ: loan of fungible articles.
qarḍ hasan: interest-free loan.
qiyās: analogy; analogical deduction.

rabb al-māl: investor; beneficial owner; sleeping partner.
riba: unlawful advantage by way of excess or deferment.
ribāwī: susceptible of *riba*.
riba al-faḍl: *riba* by way of increase or excess.
riba al-jāhiliyya: pre-Islamic *riba*.

riba al-nāsi'a: *riba* by way of deferment.
riba jalī: manifest *riba*.
riba khafī: hidden *riba*.

ṣadaqa: voluntary alms-giving.
ṣaḥīḥ: valid.
ṣarf: exchange (of two currencies).
sharīʿa: the sacred law of Islam.
sharika: partnership.
sharikat aʿmāl: labour partnership.
sharikat ʿaqd: contractual partnership.
sharikat māl: finance partnership.
sharikat mulk: proprietary partnership.
sharikat wujūh: credit partnership.
shurūt: special conditions; legal formularies.
suftaja: bill of exchange.
ṣulḥ: amicable settlement.
sunna: deeds, utterances and tacit approvals of the Prophet.
sūra: chapter of the Qur'ān.

taʿaddin: violation of trust.
taghrīr: misrepresentation.
takāful: mutual responsibility; mutual guarantee.
ṭalāq: Islamic divorce; repudiation.
taṣarruf: the dealing with (a property).
taṣarrufāt fiʿliyya: torts (offences and technical offences).
taṣarrufāt qawliyya: legal transactions (contracts and unilateral transactions).
thamaniyya: currency.
ṭuʿam: foodstuffs.

ujrat al-mithl: fair salary.
ʿurbūn: earnest money.
ʿurūḍ: chattels (movable properties, except money and animals).

waqf: religious endowment; setting up a religious foundation.

yasīr: slight, insignificant, immaterial.

zakāt: a tax levied on the gross assets of Muslims; its payment amounts to a religious duty.

Bibliography

Hanafi *fiqh*

Baz, Selim. *Sharh al-Majalla*, Beirut 1923.
Chéhata, C. *Théorie générale de l'obligation en droit musulman Hanéfite*. Sirey, Paris 1969.
Damad Effendi (Muhammad ibn Sulayman). *Majma' al-anhur sharh multaqa al-abhur*. 2 vols., Dar al-Tiba'at al-Amira, 1328 A.H.
al-Fatawa al-'Alamgiriyya. 6 vols., Cairo 1323 A.H.
Ibn 'Abidin. *Radd al-muhtar*. 5 vols., Dar al-Sa'ada, 1324 A.H.
al-Kasani. *Bada'i' al-sana'i' fi tartib al-shara'i'*. 7 vols., Cairo 1910.
al-Marghinani, al-Hidaya. *Sharh Bidayat al-mubtadi'*. 4 vols., Cairo 1326/7 A.H.
al-Sarakhsi. *al-Mabsut*. 30 vols., Cairo 1331 A.H.
al-Shaybani. *Sharh Kitab al-siyar al-kabir*. Cairo 1971.
al-Suyuti. *al-Jami' al-saghir*. 2 vols., 1352 A.H.
Ibn al-Himam. *Fath al-qadir sharh al-Hidaya*. 8 vols., 1315–1318 A.H.

Hanbali *fiqh*

al-Bahuti. *Kashshaf al-qina' 'an matn al-iqna'*. 6 vols., Riyadh 1394 A.H.
al-Rawd al-murbi' bi sharh zad al-mustaqni' – mukhtasar al-muqni'. 2 vols., 6th edn, Riyadh.
Sharh Muntaha al-iradat. Dar al-Fiqr, Medina n.d.
al-Ba'li. *al-Rawd al-nadi sharh kafi al-mubtadi'*. Cairo n.d.
al-Futuhi, Taqi al-Din ibn al-Najjar. *Muntaha al-iradat*. 2 vols., Cairo 1961/2.
al-Khiraqi, *Mukhtasar*. Damascus 1964.
al-Qari. *Majalat al-ahkam al-shar'iyya*. Eds. A.I. Abu Sulayman and M.I. 'Ali, 1st edn, Jeddah 1981.
Ibn al-Farra'. *al-Ahkam al-sultanniya*. Cairo, n.d.
Ibn Qayyim al-Jawziyya. *I'lam al-muwaqqi'in*. 4 vols., Beirut 1970.
Ibn Qudama, Muwaffaq al-Din. *al-Mughni*. 9 vols., Riyadh n.d.
Ibn Rajab. *al-Qawa'id*. Cairo, 1971.
Ibn Taymiyya. *al-Fatawa al-kubra*. 5 vols., Beirut 1966.

Maliki *fiqh*

al-Dasuqi, Muhammad ibn Muhammad 'Arafa. *Hashiya . . . 'ala sharh al-kabir li Abi al-Barakat . . . al-Dardir*. 4 vols., Cairo 1319 A.H.
al-Dardir. *al-Sharh al-saghir 'ala aqrab al-masalik ila madhhab al-Imam Malik*. 3 vols., Cairo 1972.

al-Hattab. *Mawahib al-jalil, sharh sayyidi Khalil*. 5 vols., Cairo 1329 A.H.
Ibn Juzay. *Qawanin al-ahkam al-shar'iyya*. Dar al-'ilm li'l-malayin, Beirut 1973.
Ibn Rushd. *Bidayat al-mujtahid wa-nihayat al-muqtasid*. 2 vols., 5th edn, Dar al-Ma'rifa, Beirut 1981.
al-Kashnawi. *Ashal al-madarik sharh irshad al-salik fi fiqh imam al-a'imma Malik*. 3 vols., 2nd edn, Beirut n.d.
Malik Ibn Anas. *al-Muwatta'*. Beirut 1979.
al-Qayrawani, Ibn Abi Zayd. *al-Risala, ou Traîté abrégé de droit Malékite et morale Musulmane*. Trans. Fagnan, Paris 1914.
al-Zurqani. *Sharh al-Muwatta'*. 4 vols., Dar al-Ma'rifa, Beirut 1978.

Shafii *fiqh*

al-Ghazali. *al-Mustasfa*. 2 vols., Cairo 1937.
al-Haythami. *al-Fatawa al-kubra al-fighiyya*. al-Maktaba al-Islamiyya, n.d.
al-Mawardi. *al-Ahkam al-sultaniyya*. 1st edn, Misr 1960.
Muhammad Ibn Muhammad. *al-Wajiz fi madhhab al-Imam al-Shafi'i*. Cairo, 1317 A.H.
al-Muzni. *Mukhtasar*. Dar al-Ma'rifa, Beirut n.d.
al-Nawawi. *al-Majmu', Sharh al-Muhadhdhab*. 12 vols., Cairo 1344/5 A.H. (In margin, al-Rafii's *Fath al-'aziz*.)
Minhaj al-talibin. Trans. by E. C. Howard, Lahore 1914.
Minhaj al-talibin. Trans. by L. W. C. Van Berg, 1882.
al-Shafi'i. *al-Umm*. 8 vols., Dar al-Ma'rifa, Beirut 1973.
al-Shirazi. *al-Muhadhdhab*. 2 vols., Cairo 1343 A.H.
al-Shirbini, al-Khatib. *Mughni al-muhtaj*. 4 vols., Cairo 1308 A.H.

Ibadi *fiqh*

'Abd al-'Aziz ibn al-Hajj Ibrahim al-Mus'abi al-Isgeni. *al-Nil*. 22 parts, Algiers.
Atfish, Shaikh Muhammad ibn Yusuf. *Sharh al-Nil wa shifa' al-'alil*. 10 vols., Cairo 1343 A.H.
al-Basyani. *Mukhtasar al-Basyawi*. Oman 1397 A.H.
al-Harithi. *al-'Uqud al-fidiyya fi usul al-ibadiyya*. Dar al-yaqza al-'arabiyya, Beirut n.d.
Ibn Baraka. *al-Jami'*. Cairo, 1971.
al-Maamiry, Ahmed Hamoud. *Oman and Ibadism*. Lancers, India, 1980.
Mercier, Marcel. *Etude sur le Waqf Abadhite*. Algiers, 1927.
al-Salimi. *Jawhar al-nizam fi 'ilmay al-adyan wa'l-ahkam*. al-Matba'a al-'arabiyya, Cairo 1344 A.H.
Jawhar al-nizam fi 'ilmay al-adyan wa'l-ahkam. 4 vols., edn revised by Ibrahim Atfish, Misr n.d.
Sharh Tal'at al-shams 'ala al-alafiyat. 2 vols., Misr *c*. 1317 A.H.
al-Shammakhi, 'Amir ibn 'Ali. *al-Idah*. 4 vols., Libya 1971.
Zeys, E. *Législation Mozabite*. Algiers, 1886.

Islamic law and economics

Aghnides, N. *Mohammedan Theories of Finance*. Lahore
Ahmad, Khalid. *al-Tafkir al-iqtisadi fi 'l-Islam*. Dar al-da'wa al-islamiyya, Beirut 1397 A.H.

Ahmad, Khurshid. *Studies in Islamic Economics*. King ʿAbdul ʿAziz University, Jeddah, and The Islamic Foundation, Leicester 1981.
ʿAli, Muazzam (ed.). *Islamic Banks and Strategies of Economic Co-operation*. New Century, London 1982.
Amin, Ahmad. *Fajr al-Islam*. Beirut 1969.
Arin, Félix. *Opérations usuraires et aléatoires en droit musulman*. A. Pedone, Paris 1909.
Babalbali, Mahmud. *al-Mal fi 'l-Islam*. Beirut 1975.
Cardahi, C. *Droit et morale*. 2 vols., Beirut 1954.
Colling, Alfred. *Banques et banquiers de Babylone à Wall Street*. Plon, Paris 1962.
Coulson, N. *Conflicts and Tensions in Islamic Jurisprudence*. University of Chicago Press, 1969.
A History of Islamic Law. Edinburgh University Press, 1978.
Commercial Law in the Gulf States. Graham and Trotman, 1984.
Daoualibi, M. "La théorie de l'usure en droit musulman," in *Travaux de la Semaine Internationale de Droit Musulman*. Sirey, France 1953.
Dar al Maal al Islami and Islamic Economic and Financial Institutions. New Century, London 1982.
Draz, Shaikh. "L'usure en droit musulman", in *Travaux de la Semaine Internationale de Droit Musulman*. Sirey, France 1953.
Fatawa al-Imam Muhammad Rashid Rida. Eds. Munjid, S. and Khuri, Y. Dar al-kitab al-jadid. 5 vols., Beirut 1970.
Gibb, H. A. R. and Kramers, J. H. (eds.). *A Shorter Encyclopaedia of Islam*. Brill and Luzac, Netherlands 1961.
Herbo, Ibrahim Fadil Yusuf. *ʿAqd al-mudaraba*. Iraq 1973.
Hitti, P. *Islam, A Way of Life*. Oxford University Press, 1970.
ʿItr, Nur al-Din. *al-Muʿamalat al-masrafiyya wa 'l-ribawiyya*. Risala, Beirut 1977.
Jaziri, ʿAbd al-Rahman. *al-Fiqh ʿala al-madhahib al-arbaʿa*. 5 vols., Dar Ihya' al-turath al-ʿarabi, Beirut (Vol. I: 3rd edn, n.d.; Vols. II and III, 6th edn, n.d.; Vol. IV, 1963; Vol. V, 1st edn, n.d.)
Kamel, Ibrahim. *Islamic Banks and Strategies of Economic Co-operation*. New Century, London 1982.
Khaddouri, M. and Liebesny, H. J. (eds.). *Law in the Middle East*. The Middle East Institute, Washington, D.C. 1955.
Khafif, ʿAli. *Ahkam al-muʿamalat al-sharʿiyya*. Cairo 1941.
Khan, M. Akram. *Issues in Islamic Economics*. Lahore 1983.
Kharrufa, A. *al-Riba wa'l-fa'ida*. Baghdad 1962.
Lammens, H. *La Mecque á la veille de l'Hégire*. Beirut 1924.
Mahmasani, S. *The General Theory of the Law of Obligations and Contracts under Islamic Jurisprudence*. 2 vols., Beirut 1972.
Falsafat al-tashriʿ fi 'l-Islam. Dar al-ʿilm li'l-malayin, Beirut 1975.
al-Awzaʿi. Dar al-ʿilm li'l-malayin, Beirut 1978.
Mannan, M. A. *Islamic Economics, Theory and Practice*. Lahore 1975.
al-Masri. *al-Tijara fi 'l-Islam*. Cairo 1976.
Milliot, L. *Introduction á l'étude du droit musulman*. Sirey, Paris 1971.
Muslehuddin, M. *Insurance and Islamic Law*. Reprint, New Delhi 1982.
Naqvi, S. N. H. *Ethics and Economics: an Islamic Synthesis*. The Islamic Foundation, Leicester 1981.
Qureshi, Anwar Iqbal. *Islam and the Theory of Interest*. Ashraf, Lahore 1974.
Rahim, Abdur. *Muhammadan Jurisprudence*. Lahore 1970.
Rahman, Afzallur. *Banking and Insurance*. Muslim Schools Trust, London 1979.
Rodinson, Maxime. *Islam and Capitalism*. Allen Lane, London 1974.

Rosenthal, F. *Gambling in Islam*. Brill, 1975.
Saleh, N. *The General Principles of Saudi Arabian and Omani Company Laws*. Namara, United Kingdom 1981.
Saleh, S. *Commercial Arbitration in the Arab Middle East*. Graham and Trotman, 1984.
Sanhuri, ʿAbd al-Razzaq. *Masadir al-haqq fi 'l-fiqh al-islami*. 6 vols., al-Majmaʿ al-ʿArabi al-Islami, Beirut n.d.
Schacht, J. *The Origins of Muhammadan Jurisprudence*. Clarendon Press, 1979.
al-Sharif, Sharaf ibn ʿAli. *al-Ijara al-warida ʿala ʿamal al-insan*. Saudi Arabia 1980.
Siddiqi, M. N. *Muslim Economic Thinking*. The Islamic Foundation, Leicester 1981.
Banking without Interest. The Islamic Foundation, Leicester 1983.
Issues in Islamic Banking. The Islamic Foundation, Leicester 1983.
Udovitch, A. *Partnership and Profit in Medieval Islam*. Princeton University Press, 1970.
Vesey-Fitzgerald, S. *Muhammadan Law*. Scientia, Germany, repr. 1979.
Wakin, J. *The Function of Documents in Islamic Law*. State University of New York Press, Albany 1972.
Zaydan, ʿAbd al-Karim. *Ahkam al-dhimmiyin wa'l-musta'manin*. Baghdad 1963.

Index

Names beginning with 'al-' are indexed under the next part of the name.

'Abduh, Muhammad, 28
'Abdullah Ibn Salam, 11
Abu 'l-Faraj, 74
Abu Hanifa, 23, 55, 61, 71, 72, 77, 83, 96, 98; teaching on loan contracts, 37, 42; teaching on *mudaraba*, 105, 106
Abu Hurayra, 11
Abu Yusuf, 37, 61–2, 96
'adam, see non-existence
agricultural products, as subject of contract, 37, 53, 59–60, 72, 85
alms-giving (*sadaqa*), 29
alms tax (*zakat*), 2, 29
'amal, see work
amana (fiduciary relationship), 105
analogy (*qiyas*), 14–15, 34
animals: sale of, 70–1, 72, 73, 75, 77, 79; as subject of loan agreement, 44
anwa', see species
arbitration clauses, 53 n. 8
'ariya (loan for use), 35
al-Awza'i, 42

Bahrain, 5
al-Bahuti, 97
banks, interest-free banking systems, 2–3, 87–91, 101, 102, 117–18
al-Baraka Group, 91
barter, 34, 48
bay' gha'ib (sale of subject-matter not visible at parties' meeting) 64, 67–71
bay' juzaf (sale where one of the countervalues is determined by mere viewing), 65, 76–9
bay' salam (sale with advance payment for future delivery), 21, 23, 43, 53, 59, 64, 65, 70, 71–6
Bilal, 19
bill of exchange (*suftaja*), 42, 43, 81–2, 88
Bocchoris, King of Egypt, 8

Charlemagne, Emperor, 9
chattels (*'urud*), 41, 75–6, 93; as *mudaraba* investment, 105, 111
Christian attitudes on interest, 9
Code of Hammurabi, 8
commenda partnership, *see mudaraba*
commodity exchanges, 90
consensus (*ijma'*), 12, 71
contract of manufacture, *see istisna'*
Cooper, R., 87
Coulson, N., 44
credit sale, 64, 65–7
currency (*thamaniyya*), 15, 16, 21–2, 24, 25, 65, 78, 104–5; as price in a sale contract, 62–3, 73, 75, 76, 77; as subject of loan agreement, 38–9, 40

Daoualibi, M., 29
Dar al-Harb, 30, 31
Dar al-Islam, 30, 31
Dar al Maal al Islami (D.M.I.), 90
Dar al-Sulh, 30, 31
darura, see necessity
debt, 93, 105; *see also hawalat al-dayn*
Denmark, Islamic Bank International in, 88
dhimma, 81, 105
divorce, Islamic (*talaq*), 57
donations, 56
Draz, Shaikh, 29–30
Dubai Islamic Bank, 87

earnest money, payment of, 67
Egypt, 8, 28, 87
Egyptian Civil Code, 3, 6
equity (*istihsan*), 55, 61, 98
exchanged countervalues, 45, 48; avoiding want of knowledge concerning characteristics and quantities of, 51, 52, 63–79; avoiding want of knowledge concerning existence of, 52–63; keeping effective control over, 52, 79–84; and *riba*, 13–26 *passim*, 34

Faisal Islamic Bank of Sudan, 94
fiduciary relationship (*amana*), 105
foodstuffs (*tuʿam*), as subject-matter of transaction, 15–25 *passim*, 73, 74, 75; *see also* agricultural products; fruits
Freedom of Contract, 115, 117
French legal system, influence of, 5, 6, 103
fruits, sale of, 53, 56, 59–60, 74, 75
fundamentalism, Islamic, 4, 6
al-Furuq (al-Qarafi), 50, 51
al-Futuhi, Taqi al-Din ibn al-Najjar, 92

genus (*jins*), 13, 14, 15–19 *passim*, 34
gharar (uncertainty, risk, speculation), 3–4, 5, 6, 49–85, 86, 100, 105, 108, 116, 118; definition of, 50–2; sources of prohibition of, 85; *see also* want of knowledge
al-Ghazali, 2
ghubn, see lesion
gold and silver, 14, 15–16, 20–5 *passim*, 27, 104
gratuitous contracts, 56–9
Greeks, ancient, views on interest, 8–9

Hadith (Prophet's Tradition), 13, 14, 15, 18, 19, 48
haja, see need
Hanafis, 48, 63, 86; and avoidance of want of knowledge concerning characteristics and quantities of exchanged countervalues, 65, 66, 67, 68–9, 72, 77, 78; and effects of *gharar* on donation and power of attorney, 56, 57; and *hawalat al-dayn*, 82, 83; and *ijara* (lease contract), 97; interpretaton of *ʿilla* and genus, 15, 16–17; and *istisnaʿ* (contract of manufacture), 62; and loan contracts, 35, 36, 37–8, 41, 44–5; and *mudaraba*, 104–9 *passim*, 111, 112, 113; and *murabaha*, 96; and partnership, 92, 93; and *riba*, 19–21, 31; and sale of fruits and agricultural products, 59, 60
Hanbalis, 2, 4, 5; and avoidance of want of knowledge concerning countervalues' characteristics, 63, 65, 66, 67, 68, 70, 74–5, 78–9; and effects of *gharar* on gratuitous contracts and unilateral transactions, 56, 58; and *hawalat al-dayn*, 82; and *ijara* (lease contract), 98; interpretation of *ʿilla* and genus, 15–16, 17; and *istisnaʿ* (contract of manufacture), 62; and loan contracts, 35, 38–9, 41–2, 45; and *mudaraba*, 104, 105, 106, 108, 111, 112, 113, 114; and *murabaha*, 96; and *riba*, 22–4, 31; and sale of fruits and agricultural products, 60
haqq al-khiyar, see option, right of
Hassan, Zaydan Abu al-Karim, 30
hawalat al-dayn (assignment of debt), 81–4
hire contracts, 54–5, 59, 97, 104; *see also ijara wa-iqtina*
hiyal (legal stratagems), 36, 48, 86, 95, 117

Ibadis, 4, 7; and avoidance of want of knowledge concerning countervalues' existence and characteristics, 53, 60, 62, 65, 67, 70, 71, 75–6, 79; and effects of *gharar* on gratuitous contracts and unilateral transactions, 56, 57, 58; and *hawalat al-dayn*, 82, 83; and *ijara* (lease contract), 98; interpretation of *ʿilla* and genus, 16, 18; and loan contracts, 40–1, 43–4, 46; and *mudaraba*, 104, 105, 106, 108, 109, 111, 113, 114; and *murabaha*, 96; and partnership, 92, 93, 94; and *riba*, 26, 31
ibdaʿ (remittance of capital for trading on the understanding that profits go to the capitalist), 109
Ibn ʿAbbas, ʿAbdullah, 26–7, 30
Ibn Abi Layla, 96
Ibn Hanbal, Ahmad, 15, 67, 71, 83, 97, 98, 106
Ibn Juzay, 51
Ibn Qayyim al-Jawziyya, 2, 13, 16, 27, 50, 53, 54
Ibn Qudama, Muwaffaq al-Din, 38, 41, 42, 75, 80, 92; on genus and species, 15–16, 17; on *gharar*, 56, 71; on *riba al-fadl*, 22
Ibn Rushd, 21, 51, 53, 72, 73, 80, 97
Ibn Taimiyya, 27
ijara (lease contract), 89, 97–9
ijara wa-iqtinaʾ (hire purchase contract), 89, 99
ijmaʿ, *see* consensus
ʿilla (efficient cause), 13, 14–16, 17, 19–26 *passim*, 34
ʿinan (limited investment partnership), 92–4
ʿinan sharikat aʿmal (finance-limited partnership), 93–4
insurance, 5, 28, 50, 86, 100
interest, 3; early views on, 8–12; *see also riba*
interest-free banks, *see* banks
investment companies, 90, 102, 117, 118
Islamic Bank International, 88
Islamic Companies Code, 87
Islamic financial institutions, 90–1
Islamic schools of law, 12, 14, 34; *see also* Hanafis; Hanbalis; Ibadis; Malikis; Shafiis; Zahiris
istihsan, *see* equity
istisnaʿ (contract of manufacture), 53, 59, 61–2, 104

jahl, *see* want of knowledge
Jamal al-Din al-Afghani, Saiyid, 28
Jewish laws on interest, 9, 10–11
jins, *see* genus
Justinian, Emperor of Rome, 9

khiyar al-ru'ya (option after inspection), 61, 67–8, 69
Kuwait, 4, 5–6
Kuwait Finance House, 91

Layth ibn Sa'd, 39
lease contract, *see ijara*
Lebanon, Lebanese, 5, 103
lesion (*ghubn*), 52, 116
life assurance, 100
loan, 35, 65; *see also 'ariya*; *qard*; *qard hasan*

Mahmasani, Subhi, 54
mal ribawi (property susceptible of *riba*), 13, 65, 66
Malik ibn Anas, 38, 71, 79, 80, 83, 98, 106
Malikis: and avoidance of want of knowledge concerning countervalues' existence and characteristics, 59, 60, 63, 65, 66, 67, 68, 69–70, 73–4, 77–8; and effects of *gharar* on gratuitous contracts and unilateral transactions, 56, 57–8; and *hawalat al-dayn*, 82, 83; and *ijara* (lease contract), 98; interpretation of *'illa* and genus, 16, 18; and *istisna'* (contract of manufacture), 62; and loan contracts, 35, 39, 42–3, 45–6; and *mudaraba*, 104, 105, 106, 108, 110–11, 112, 113; and *murabaha*, 95, 97; and partnership, 92, 93; and *riba*, 24–5, 31
al-Manar, 28
manfa'a, *see* use
manufacture, contract of, *see istisna'*
manumission (*'itq*), 57
Mecca, Meccan period, 1–2, 9–10, 12, 34
Medina, Medinan period, 1, 2, 10, 11, 12
Mit Ghamr, Egypt, establishment of Islamic bank in, 87
money markets, international, 90
mudaraba (commenda partnership), 3, 4, 11, 29, 88, 89, 90, 91, 92, 99, 101–14; capital, 104–6; definition of, 103–4; liquidation of, 110–11, 112; rights and duties of agent-managers, 107–8, 109–14; rights and duties of investors, 106–9; solidarity *mudaraba*, 100
mufawada (unlimited equal partnership), 92, 93, 94
Muhajirun, 11
Muhammad (the Prophet), 1, 9, 10, 11, 23, 43, 49, 55, 71; and prohibition of *gharar*, 85; on *riba*, 19, 34, 37
Muhammad, disciple of Abu Hanifa, 37
Muhammad 'Abduh, 28
murabaha (cost-plus-profit contract), 89, 91, 94–7
musharaka (partnership, participation financing), 89, 91–4, 99

Nasser Social Bank, 87
naw', *see* species
necessity (*darura*), 42, 53, 55, 76, 98; *darura mulji'a* or *mulihha* (pressing necessity), 27, 29
need (*haja*), 27, 29, 36, 53
Nicaea, First Council of, 9
non-existence (*'adam*) of subject-matter in transaction, 52–4, 57, 59, 61, 85
North Yemen, *see* Yemen Arab Republic

Oman, 4, 5, 7, 103
option, right of (*haqq al-khiyar*), 61 n. 55, 77, 116; *see also khiyar al-ru'ya*

Pakistan, 32, 87
participation financing, 91, 94; *see also musharaka*
partnership, 91–4; *see also mudaraba*; *musharaka*
power of attorney, 55, 57–8
price, 80–4; avoiding want of knowledge with regard to, 51, 52, 62–3, 66
profit-sharing systems, 3
Prophet's Companions, 11, 26–7, 30
Prophet's Tradition, *see* Hadith

qard (loan of fungible commodities), 35–48, 108; repayment of, according to *fiqh*, 37–44; and *riba*, 35–7; validity of, with a *riba* stipulation, 44–7; *see also qard hasan*
qard hasan (interest-free loan), 89, 99–100
Qatar, 5
qiyas, *see* analogy
Quran, 1–2, 55; prohibition of *gharar* in, 49, 85; prohibition of *riba* in, 9–12, 13, 33–4, 48

al-Rajii Group, 91
Rashid Rida, Muhammad, 28
repudiation (Islamic divorce, *talaq*), 57
riba, 1, 2, 3–4, 5–7, 8–34, 47–8, 65, 95; definition of, 13–14; and Islamic financial system, 86–91, 99; and loan contracts, 35–7, 44–7; manifest (*riba jali*) and hidden (*riba khafi*), 27, 28; Quranic doctrine on, 9–12, 13, 33–4, 48; and Sharia Law of Contract, 116, 117, 118; sources of prohibition of, 33–4;

riba – cont.
traditional and other views on, 19–30; in transactions with non-Muslims, 30–2; *see also riba al-fadl*; *riba al-jahiliyya*; *riba al-nasi'a*
riba al-fadl (*riba* by way of excess), 13, 27, 28, 29, 36, 63–4; views of schools of law on, 19, 20, 21, 22–3, 24
riba al-jahiliyya (pre-Islamic *riba*), 13, 27, 28, 29, 30, 36
riba al-nasi'a (*riba* by way of deferment), 13, 36, 48, 64, 66, 72, 73, 74, 75; traditional views on, 19–29 *passim*
risk, commercial, 64, 116; *see also gharar*
Rodinson, Maxime, 12
Romans, ancient, attitudes on interest, 8–9

sadaqa (voluntary alms-giving), 29
Sahnun, 74
Salafiyya party, 28
sale, 34, 48, 49, 50, 51, 64–5, 79–80, 85; *bayʿ al-hasah*, 51, 85; *bayʿ muhaqala*, 85; *bayʿ mukhadara*, 85; *bayʿ mulamasa*, 51, 85; *bayʿ munabadha*, 51, 85; as way of assessing quality of articles, 19; *see also bayʿ gha'ib*; *bayʿ juzaf*; *bayʿ salam*; credit sale
al-Salimi, 16
Sanhuri, ʿAbd al-Razzaq, 3, 8, 28–9, 36, 51, 54
sarf (exchange of two currencies), 21–2, 24, 25, 65
Saudi Arabia, 4, 5, 6, 103
savings bank accounts, 28
Schacht, J., 10
seasonal articles, sale of, 75
service charges, bank, 88
al-Shafiʿi, 23, 39, 42, 71, 77, 83, 98, 105, 106
Shafiis, 4, 48, 86; avoidance of want of knowledge concerning countervalues' existence and characteristics, 53, 60, 63, 65, 66, 67, 68, 72–3, 78; and effects of *gharar* on gratuitous contracts and unilateral transactions, 56, 58; and *ijara* (lease contract), 97–8; interpretation of *ʿilla* and genus, 15, 16, 17; and *istisnaʿ* (contract of manufacture), 62; and loan contracts, 35, 36, 39–40, 43, 46–7; and *mudaraba*, 104, 105, 107, 108, 111, 112, 113, 114; and *murabaha*, 96, 97; and partnership, 92, 93, 94; and *riba*, 21–2, 23, 25, 31
al-Shammakhi, ʿAmir ibn ʿAli, 16, 18, 52, 70, 76, 79, 96, 98
Sharia (sacred law of Islam), 2–5 *passim*, 6, 35–6, 89, 91, 103–4
Sharia Law of Contract, 115–18
sharikat aʿmal (labour partnership), 92, 93–4
sharikat ʿaqd (contractual partnership), 91
sharikat mal (finance partnership), 92
sharikat mulk (property partnership), 91
sharikat wujuh (credit partnership), 92
shurut, *see* special conditions
Siddiqi, M. N., 95
solidarity companies, 91
Solon, 9
special conditions (*shurut*) in contracts, 44–7, 115 n. 2
species (*anwaʿ*), 13, 14, 17, 18
speculation, *see gharar*
Sudan, 87, 94
suftaja, *see* bill of exchange
Sunna, 1, 34, 53
Syria, 5

takaful (mutual guarantee), 89, 100–1
talaq (Islamic divorce), 57
talaqi al-rukban, 49
thamaniyya, *see* currency
tuʿam, *see* foodstuffs
Tunisia, 5
Twelve Tables (of ancient Rome), 9

uncertainty, *see gharar*
unilateral transactions, 56–9
ʿurud, *see* chattels
use (*manfaʿa*), as subject-matter of transaction, 54–5, 59, 97–8

want of knowledge (*jahl*), 46, 51, 98, 100; avoidance of, concerning characteristics and quantities of exchanged countervalues, 51, 52, 63–79; avoidance of, concerning existence of exchanged countervalues, 52–63
waqf (religious endowment), 57
wills, 57
wine, drinking of, 1, 2, 14
work (*ʿamal*), as subject-matter of contract, 54, 59

Yemen Arab Republic, 4, 5, 103

Zahiris, 15, 34
Zaidi school of law, 4
zakat (alms tax), 2, 29